ATOMIC STEPS

FROM A NEGATIVE MINDSET TO A
POSITIVE MINDSET THROUGH A
SEVEN-DAY PROCESS FOR LIFELONG
BENEFITS

LAWRENCE CONTI

The Journey to Self-Illumination Series

npp

NORDEN PACIFIC PRESS-NORDEN PACIFIC LLC

This book is dedicated to my family, especially my mother, who is currently reading it in heaven.
As a result of twenty years of strokes, she had lost her ability to speak, so when she attempted to motivate me, she would grasp my hand tightly with her weakened left hand in order to convey her message.
Without any conversation, but through her perceptive glance, we already understood each other. She has always been proud of me, and she should be even more so now.
Thanks for her first storybook to me about Dream.

With my genuine gratitude to the following heroes behind me:

C.J., Christian, Cori, Dane, Frankie, Hayley, Jack, Jana, Karen, Lauren, Nina, Sophie, Virginie

BELIEVE

NEXTGEN AND ANCIENT WISDOM

Ancient Greek: Ἄτομος (Atomos)
The smallest elements of the universe—Democrates

Contemporary Science: Atomic Steps
Tiny one-atom-tall steps that are "present on nearly all crystal surfaces" (Henzler, 1976) that resemble the "staircase in a house" (Fedina & Latyshev, 2015)

Ancient Chinese Wisdom:
A Journey of a thousand miles begins with a single step.

CONTENTS

WELCOME ABOARD! HERE'S A BOARDING PASS TO A JOURNEY OF ATOMIC STEPS

Airport terminals offer me three choices. I can fret about delays, deepening my inner darkness; I can unfold my mobile office to curate my latest business deals, elevating my stress-levels; or I can take one step, one atomically small step, closer to clarity.

The flight will arrive. The deals will go through. I'll land on the other side, a happier, nicer human.

This book is about my adventures in taking *Atomic Steps* in pursuit of a positive mindset.

I just asked Siri to play me one of my inspiring songs by Bobby McFerrin because it fits my mood perfectly:

Don't worry, be happy

And now I'm smiling at the cabin crew as I take my seat on my latest journey. Come with me on this relaxing trip!

WHEN THE HALF-EMPTY GLASS IS ACTUALLY EMPTY

The old saying is that pessimists see the glass as half empty while optimists see it as half full. For many people in our fractured times, however, the glass *is actually empty!*

OK. So let's start with that empty glass. Pick it up and run your fingers over its smooth surfaces. Here's a strange fact you might not know, though. Glass is semi-liquid. It behaves strangely, unlike other solids. On the other hand, however, like other crystals, the surfaces of its components are actually slightly inclined, with a set of all-but-invisible "atomic steps" leading from a low side to a high side. Atomic steps are the imperceptible, one-atom-high steps on the apparently smooth face of a crystal. And that gets us into what I have experienced and what I will describe.

Escaping negativity is not about climbing high, difficult steps—it is about taking many simple steps repeatedly. The best way to change from negative to positive is incrementally over time.

My problem is that I am a businessman without any special guru superpowers. I admire the tranquility of those who opt out of the world and its challenges, but I am no full-time mystic. Many books have been written about inner peace and a positive mindset. I have read many of them. They do not match my personality and lifestyle, though. I love the adventure of the business world, and I am committed to making the world a better place through my entrepreneurial skills. One of my tasks is to share with you the insights I have gained into positivity. This is not a book for those who are at leisure to take giant strides towards tranquility. It is a book for those who, like me, need a more relaxed approach to the process. My way is the gentle way of small steps and tiny increments that lead, cumulatively, to a lifestyle of great brightness!

I am sharing this from my heart. This book is not designed to draw you into an expensive seminar or coaching course in which I will share the "deeper and better" stuff. What you see is what you get! I'm here, sharing my thoughts and experiences with my friends. If I think of anything else, I'll just write another book.

One observation I make everywhere I travel is that so many people seem to be locked into a negative mindset. They can't escape the vortex of gloom and depression. They *want* to get out! Nobody thrives on angry thoughts and obsessive fears. If you are there, then you know what I mean. Somehow, however, you can't seem to let those negative experiences go. They gnaw at you and leave you no peace. Trivial complaints and shapeless fears monopolize your thoughts: The food is too salty; the weather is too wet; the traffic is always wrong; my colleagues set traps for me; my spouse might be having an affair with someone; I can't achieve my goals; I'll fail my next assessment... Negativity is like a python coiling around your body, tightening its deadly grip each time you breathe out.

Stop struggling. No, I don't want you to suffocate to death. On the contrary, I want you to breathe fresh air again. Escaping strangling negativity is not about putting out huge amounts of energy. You don't *have* huge amounts of energy. Escaping from negativity only requires small, low-energy steps. As you take one atomic step after another, the negativity will fall back. You might feel it breathing down your neck, but horses only have to win by a neck! Yes, negativity is close behind you. "Behind you" is the key. The coils of your negative mindset will magically release their grip as you move *away* from negativity rather than *towards* it. I have found a workable, practical way for even a hyper-committed businessperson to get out of their inner darkness.

If you are anything like me, you have done all the courses, am I right? You have read so many books and attended expensive seminars. Always, the disappointment sets in when you take your next business trip or attend your next class. The schemes are too complex. The ideas are not clear. You agree that something must be done, but you have no clarity about what steps to take. Or else, the steps you are asked to do will require more energy than you have. The path ahead is steep and rough, and it would take a spiritual giant to go that way. Well, fortunately, I'm not a spiritual giant, just an ordinary human being making the best of my way through life. And I have discovered a path with only atomically small steps. Walk with me for a bit and see if it suits you.

The people in your life have not helped you to tackle this issue of inner negativity, either. Friends have poured scorn on your efforts and bombarded you with cynical dismissals of your desires to live a more positive life. Trapped in their own negativity, they try to get you to buy into their defeatist outlook. On the other hand, your family has told you to buck up, apply more willpower, and stop sulking. That hasn't helped you at all, especially as you can see that they often can't follow their own advice. You've seen the doctor, consumed the vitamins, and tried all the diets. You find yourself still stuck in negativity. Not only is your glass not half empty, it's completely empty. Dammit, the glass is "broken," and you have "cut" yourself on the shards of your broken life.

You might be one of the millions of desperate people who have listened to advertising and started taking vitamins or other supplements. I'm not putting down modern medicine or herbal remedies that have been used for years. Medicines serve a purpose. But they don't seem to be doing much if you have a bathroom cabinet full of half-empty bottles of different supplements. It looks like all you have done is make your urine worth more money (these options are not cheap). That is exactly what supplements are. They add to how you deal with bad things as a whole. Maybe you thought that taking all those pills would make you feel better, even if it was just a placebo effect, but you are too smart for that to work. They can't make you happy on their own; at best, they can help the process. If you can't live without this help, you need a supplement to your supplements! I suggest a step-by-step approach with atomic steps.

I'm not here to judge you or condemn you. I myself have been stuck at times, hardly able to fulfill the most basic requirements in life, let alone taking any active steps out of darkness. I do not have any great expectations of you, but I do have great good will towards you. I do not mind how deep you have sunk into negativity, and I am not asking any questions. I accept you as you are now. You owe me no explanations, and I don't want any. I am simply a fellow traveler on these difficult paths, and this is my very own "little way." If you are just an average human, then I'm also one!

I have spent a lifetime under high pressure in the business world, so many of my insights come from the travel stresses and insights that have come to me on my journeys. This is very appropriate for this material because we are all on a journey through life. As I reflect on my achievements, I realize that I've stumbled on a simple way of coping with negativity in life that I badly want to share with others. "Don't worry, be happy" might sound simplistic, too facile to really be of much use. It catches two important moves, however—moving *away* from the negative means moving *towards* the positive.

Come and join me on what I will call the journey.

We'll start this journey with some reflection on what this negative mindset is and why it's so important not to passively give in to it.

SUMMARY

- Ordinary humans need a simpler rule of life than vocational mystics.
- Being stuck in a negative mindset is a very common issue.

- People often get bad advice and discouragement from friends and family.
- We all need a friend who does not judge us.
- This book presents a simple, doable approach to moving away from negativity and toward positivity.

PART ONE
WHY ATOMIC STEPS WORK

First, we need to work through some misunderstandings about how to emerge from the negative into a positive mindset. It's simpler than you might expect!

CHAPTER 1

THE DARK DIMENSIONS IN YOUR MIND (AND THE WAY OUT YOU NEVER KNEW!)

INSIGHT: THE DARKEST PATH

The soldier walked along the ancient elephant path with one finger resting nervously on the trigger. There was no moon that night. The sand underfoot faintly reflected the starlight. He and his companions were hemmed in by impenetrable thorny scrub. Even elephants could not force a new path through it. The only path was kept open by the great animals down the millennia, a highway for all the deadly animals of the night, lions, leopards, and hippopotamuses.

The great path-keeping elephants themselves could dismissively brush aside a puny human with one sweep of their trunk, trampling their broken remains almost without noticing. The soldier knew that every animal was overpowering. His heart was pounding in his chest, and he could hear it beating from the echo in his eardrums. The hairs on the back of his neck were raised, and his palms were slippery with sweat. His heart was pounding in his chest. He kept his finger steady on the trigger. He hoped he could get off a single shot in time.

How dark is the path you are on in life? My friend the soldier describes how that kilometer-long stretch of path seemed like an eternity long. Taking one step at a time, however, he got through into the safety of open scrubland.

Come with me on a journey from the dark to the light, from deep negativity to open positivity. Take the next atomic step. First, though, it is essential to deal with a difficulty we all face: Paralysis.

OVERCOMING PARALYSIS

I don't take this for granted. The next step is often the very thing we can't do! Part of the problem of a negative mindset is that it often paralyzes us.

Insight From Deadline Stress

I remember being paralyzed once, like a deer in the headlights. I was working as a junior member of a team assembling a quote for a major contract that would bring in substantial income. I was assigned the research and development of a cost analysis for a highly technical aspect of the quote. It was incredibly hard to get down to the task. The deadline came closer and closer, and I had nothing. Looking back, I can see how negativity held me back. I was afraid I would make mistakes. I deeply doubted that I was competent to do the research. I felt inferior to everyone else on the team. I felt sick to my stomach with anxiety every time I entered the office. I was terrified that I would not be able to present anything at all. I was convinced I would lose my job.

I was rescued by a legal secretary, an older black woman with a calm, confident smile. She had seen many new executives come and go. She stopped me by the coffee machine and asked me straight out, "How's that research, Lawrence? It needs to be on my desk for editing tomorrow." I could not raise my eyes to look at her. She knew immediately that I was in a crisis. I will never forget what she said to me.

"Take a step back. Breathe. You can do this if you break it down into small pieces"

"What small pieces?" I choked out. "It's too complex."

"Oh, don't worry," she smiled. "Let me show you exactly how small. First step, come and sit down at your desk with that cup of coffee." I followed her mutely to my desk.

"There!" she said, "was that small enough?" I laughed weakly. "I guess so," I said.

"Next step," said my unexpected life coach, "turn on your computer." I did so, sheepishly.

"Step three: open Excel," she went on. "Are you getting the hang of it yet? That's three small steps you've accomplished!"

Suddenly, a light came on. My kind friend had rewired the circuitry in my mind, and confidence surged back. "Thank you so much," I said, laughing. "I get it now!"

"Good," she said, smiling. "I have a meeting until three o'clock. I'll swing by afterwards, and you can tell me how many small steps you have taken!"

By the time she returned, I had taken 79 small steps, and my research was well under control. I was confident I could meet the deadline. My skills were more than enough to do a great job on the project.

All I had needed was that one encouraging, non-judgmental friend to encourage me to take those first few atomic steps.

I would like to be that friend for you.

THE CREEPING INFLUENCE OF A "NEGATIVE MINDSET"?

My grandmother is a serene little woman, deep in her 90s now. She can't remember what she had for lunch anymore, but boy, can she remember everything that happened in the 1940s and 1950s! She tells how she cycled to school on frosty mornings and played in the meadowlands with her friends, meadows that have long since been swallowed up by suburban sprawl. Furthermore, she recalls walking up to the university in the rain and boiling eggs on an iron in her digs. Her tales are of simpler, happier times. And science agrees with her!

Recent meta-analytic (historical) studies have demonstrated that we live in a much more stressful environment, globally, than we did in the 1950s. My grandmother's fading memory shelters her from the anxiety and depression that plague so many of my contemporaries. The American Psychological Association's Journal of Personality and Social Psychology reports (ed.) that depression and related substance abuse are spiraling out of control (APA, 2000). In January 2021, the Journal of Public Health from Oxford University Press showed us alarming figures about the post-lockdown depression and anxiety rates in the USA during the Covid-19 pandemic, which were 39% for depression and 42% for anxiety. What is compelling is that it stated that "males were more likely to have depression, and females were more likely to have anxiety symptoms" (Jagdish et al, 2021).

I don't have the luxury of my grandmother's ultra-short memory to cocoon me from the realities of life. Neither do you. So, we all need to develop effective, actionable strategies, not hi-tech approaches. Hi-tech is one of the things that raises our stress-temperatures in the first place!

THE INFECTED ROOT OF NEGATIVITY

We can't ignore the topic of positivity. A negative mindset is not just something you can live with. It will actively corrode your life.

Insight From the Dentist

Have you ever had the misfortune of hearing your dentist tell you that you need root canal treatment? I hope not! I, on the other hand, know all about it. When I was in my twenties, I went to my dentist, Dr. Walker, with terrible pain in the side of my face. This is how the process unfolds.

You report to the dentist with an ache in your jaw. He (or she—but dentists with a "feminine touch" are just as ruthless as their male counterparts!) gets you to clamp that little x-ray plate between your teeth. They snap a shot of the hidden workings of your mouth. A little serious chatter between the dentist and his assistant follows, and then the dentist hovers over you and delivers the unwanted news: "I'm sorry, sir, but this requires a root canal treatment"

The dentist explains that, unbeknownst to you, one of your older fillings has cracked. This has let bacteria in, and the root of your tooth is now under attack. The dentist prescribes antibiotics and makes a date for reconstruction work on your tooth.

Two weeks later, you are back in the chair, staring at the ceiling. The dentist injects anesthetic in a wiggly way, and the entire side of your face goes mercifully numb. Your jaw hinges creak as the process of drilling, cleaning, and embedding a piece of miniature rebar in your tooth grinds on. You get a temporary filling and another date for fitting the crown. You rinse and spit, and stagger gratefully out of the surgery.

Negativity is the infection that spreads in the roots of our lives. When a root gets infected, you really shouldn't avoid fixing it. You'll only suffer more and more, painfully.

I have already noted the "Big Three" negatives: Stress, depression, and anxiety. This does not, however, cover the whole range of infec-tions that cause us pain. It's a frightening list. Some of these have hit me hard over the years. I am sure you could identify several unique negativities that have troubled your life, and that are troubling your inner peace right now: It could also be a combination, maybe, of the following:

- Anger
- Rage
- Irritation
- Spite
- Lust for revenge
- Fear
- Anxiety
- Nervousness
- Self-doubt
- Disgust
- Racism
- Impatience
- Sadness
- Grief
- Regret
- Homesickness
- Discontent
- Shock
- Stress
- Lack of balance

And so many more.

I will discuss a lot more about this on the "Friday" of my atomic step week. For the moment, let us be aware that psychologist Paul Eckman isolated six core human emotions in the 1970s—sadness, disgust, fear, surprise, anger, and happiness. There are many other emotions that develop from combinations of these "atoms" of human experience, such as jealousy or curiosity (Cherry, 2021). Of the six basic elements of our emotional capacity, only one—happiness—automatically tends toward the positive. All our other emotions find their first focus in the negativities of our environment. The science of evolution suggests that our emotions developed to answer only one question: "How can I stay alive?" (Al-Shawaf et al.,

2015). Our lives are more than an escape from death, though, and all the emotions can indeed come to reinforce our aspirations to happiness, but that process takes many small atomic steps.

The science of the mind suggests we might all be in over our heads in negativity. We need a way out, and atomic steps will get us there!

THE DEEP DISCOMFORT OF A NEGATIVE MINDSET

When I have allowed my life to be dominated by the five negative emotions, I have experienced pain. Perhaps you can relate. When I'm rocked and jangled by hate and fear and disappointment and sorrow, I can literally not think straight. It is as distracting as physical pain—like that toothache. Pain demands attention and denies us, giving attention to anything else.

Insight From a School Yard

When I was ten years old, my pain came from a group of bullies at school. They would hit me, hold me down, steal my things, and mock me all the time. Going to school became a daily struggle. Then I realized I could join the judo society. It was a small step towards freedom.

I remember arriving at the Dojo in my clean white judo gi (Judo fighting suit) on my first day. Everybody seemed so strong and skilled. That day, I learned the forward breakfall (mae ukemi) and the back breakfall (ushiro ukemi). I watched the seniors sparring in awe. I helped roll up the tatami (mat) and pack it away. That whole week, the bullies teased me about my martial arts. It was not a good week.

The next week, I learned the right-side and left-side breakfalls (yoko ukemi). As I remember it, although the bullies continued to mock me, the physical attacks started to tail off. As a timid white belt who did not yet even know all the breakfalls. I realize now that although I had not learned much, I had taken a few atomic steps toward freedom. By stepping into the company of the fighters I admired, some of their reputations rubbed off on me. We shall see how this led me to understand the role of support we need in our small steps out of negativity.

And so I progressed. My neck and back muscles became strong. My stomach could not be easily punched in anymore. I learned the rolling forward breakfalls (mae mawari ukemi), and I started to learn the grappling techniques and throws. Stripe by stripe, I advanced to my yellow belt, then on to my orange belt and its three stripes, little by little advancing my techniques and strength. I found I had a natural aptitude for floor work and discovered the power of the Scarf hold (kese katami). I was now more than equal to responding to those attacks from the bullies. Ironically, they never came. Perhaps I had a new aura of dangerous competence? Bullies never like a fair fight.

There was eventually an attack, but it was the last. They caught me alone in the playground and surrounded me in a threatening circle. One of my tormentors, a boy named Paul, grabbed me from behind around my chest and shoulders, so the others could hit me.

Never grab a judoka like that! I wheeled him over in the air in a confident Uki Otoshi throw. I am ashamed to say I let go of him on the way down (Judoka are taught to be polite and let their opponents down gently when they have thrown them), so he crashed onto the ground with a rib-jarring thud. The circle of bullies dissolved in horror. It was my last ever playground fight!

Bullying is one of the most negative experiences a child can have. Some kids even end up committing suicide. In 18 months, by taking a long series of very small steps, I had moved from playground negativity to playground peace and positivity. This all built into my adulthood, understanding the way of atomic steps.

Not many have the aptitude to take the path I took against bullies. But anybody can take the same *sort* of path against negativity. The intensity of negativity can become the catalyst for starting on the journey to a positive mindset. The toothache drives you to the dentist. The bully drives you to the dojo (the training hall). Negativity can break itself and produce a positive outcome!

CAN ANYONE ESCAPE A NEGATIVE MINDSET?

All our negative emotions—our anger, fear, disgust, grief, and surprise—are designed to thrust us towards a path of surviving and thriving. You do not have to be an expert in anything to feel the entire range of these emotions. Nature has equipped absolutely everybody with an innate mechanism to move from darkness into the light.

Insight From a Caver

Rachel Cox was eighteen years old when her lamp malfunctioned in the winding tunnel-maze of Wind Cave, South Dakota. Darkness engulfed her, complete, utter darkness.

In 1989, Rachel was, ironically, a trainee cave rescuer. This experience was about to change her life.

Crawling back along the tunnel she thought she had just come through, she discovered that she had, in fact, chosen a slightly different route, and that led to a 30-hour ordeal. The search-and-rescue trainees struggled to find her. County spelunkers (cavers) were mobilized, along with search and rescue dogs. Rachel was completely lost in the sprawling underground network of tunnels and dead-ends.

She survived, though—but not because she was superhuman in any way.

Rachel kept moving. She had no pack, no light, no water, and no food. She did know, however, that she must keep moving or die. HypotherSteffy kills the lost. The core temperature of the body drops, the mind becomes sluggish, and quite quickly the unfortunate stray falls asleep and never wakes up again. So, she kept moving, the only way to generate enough heat to survive. Step-by-step, she kept herself alive, shouting and singing until her voice was hoarse. For thirty hours, she kept sleep and death at bay, constantly taking one atomic step at a time.

None of those single steps brought her out of darkness, but all the steps combined eventually did. A rescuer found her, and she emerged into the light. She was exhausted, dehydrated, and hallucinating—but she was alive! (Scharper, 2020)

That story makes me excited because it gives me hope that anyone can escape darkness and negativity! The only thing required are atomic steps!

THE UNDERESTIMATED DESTRUCTIVENESS OF A NEGATIVE MINDSET

Perhaps you are still paralyzed and still wondering whether you can embark on "a journey of a thousand hardly noticeable steps," as the Chinese proverb goes. Don't stress. You only need to stagger seven steps to be free.

I do need to make sure you understand how dangerous your current situation is, though. Rachel Cox knew about hypotherSteffy. I must tell you about hypo-negativity.

A negative mindset actively eats away at our well-being, which is why we need to take a few steps away from it. Medical journalist Bree Maloney writes that, "Doctors have found that people with high levels of negativity are more likely to suffer from degenerative brain diseases, cardiovascular problems, digestive issues, and recover from sickness much slower than those with a positive mindset" (Maloney, 2022).

That is not all. Tick any items on this list that might have shown up in your struggles with negativity:

- Headache
- Chest pain
- Fatigue

- Upset stomach
- Sleep problems
- Anxiety
- Depression
- Social withdrawal
- Drastic changes in metabolism (i.e., overeating or under-eating) (Maloney, 2022)

I know these old enemies too. If we remain where we are, trapped in negativity, we do not only *experience* pain, but the pain gets worse. It does not have to!

Insight From Quicksand

Outdoorsman and "primal survivor" Hazen Audel demonstrates this issue in his traumatic video on escaping quicksand. If you are unlucky enough to fall into quicksand, you cannot just stay stuck. The mud will eventually suck you under, or you will die of heat, cold, or thirst. Staying where you are is not an option.

Audel explains that powerful moves are not your friends. The slow-moving mud will not allow you to break its grip with sheer strength. The trick, he says, is to relax. Then make tiny movements, working your legs upward behind you. Make one small move and let the mud seep into the little cavity you have made. When it has seeped in, make your next small move, and after many small moves, you will find yourself stretched out on the surface in a swimming position.

At that point, you can very gradually "swim" your way over to the edge of the quicksand, and eventually lever yourself out onto solid ground. Not only are small steps the best way to extricate yourself from danger, they are the "only" steps that will save you (Audel, 2017).

As unpleasant as your negativity feels to you now, it will inevitably feel worse and worse. Misery is not containable. It will eat into your psychological, spiritual, social, and physical well-being. It will not continue in the same way.

On the other hand, you can start to wiggle your toes in the quick-sand! Just a wiggle! Just an atomic step. I'll coach you and encourage you. You are not alone.

ENTERING THE REVOLUTIONARY WARFARE AGAINST THE NEGATIVE

For more than a century, Russia has assumed that they were the revolutionaries in any conflict. In the face of their February 2022 invasion of Ukraine, however, the Ukrainians have called shotgun on the "revolutionary" title. If an armed aggressor invades your country, then loyal citizens of the invaded country should become revolutionaries.

A revolution in this sense is very positive. It is based on a sense of justice and fairness. It can involve open warfare or hidden raids. It can be carried out by ordinary citizens who support the revolutionary forces and by overseas news-media that call for support of the revolutionary cause. A long series of small actions can lead to the invaders being defeated and expelled.

The parallels with our project of moving from a negative mindset to a positive one are clear. I am inviting you to join a struggle in which many other people are already involved. The invading enemy is negativity. Our dream of a restored nation is the dream of relaxed positivity. Our warfare will be accomplished by atomic steps—but not by atomic weapons!

EATING THE ELEPHANT: THE PRINCIPLE OF ONE BITE AT A TIME

The massive carcass of the elephant lay slumped on the ground, dead.

After the company's annual seminar for its Southern Africa Region, the chairperson decided to go on a little safari along with a few of the other delegates. They were heading home reluctantly after a week in the Addo Elephant Park. They had spent an enthralling seven days shadowing elephants under the close supervision of their guide. On their way to the exit gate, they came across the scene of carnage, offering one last unique experience. Their broad-shoul-dered guide, Bhekumbuso, pulled up their all-terrain vehicle a little way off. The visitors were disturbed to see the ruin of the magnifi-cent animal.

Bekhumbuso said in his deep voice. "This is not the time to cry. See, the great one fell in a fight with another bull elephant. See behind his head."

They saw a wound about the size of a dinner-plate behind the elephant's head. "So, this isn't the work of a poacher?" One of the delegates ventured.

"No," their guide said slowly. "No man had a hand in this! This is the way of nature. The two great bulls fought. One of them swung his tusk, so!" Bekhumbuso's hand swept in a sharp semicircle. "Sometimes this is how the fight ends. Now, the great body will give life to all the rest."

The visitors realized how privileged they were to witness even this aspect of wild Africa.

"But Bhekumbuso," their chairperson asked, "where are all the lions, hyenas, and vultures?"

Bhekumbuso laughed his large laugh. "Even in death, ma'am, the other animals fear the elephant! It will take them many hours to be brave enough to come near. This happened not long ago."

At that moment, we caught a movement at the forest line. Hesi-tantly, obviously terrified, and yet obviously hungry, a small black-backed jackal came creeping up to the vast bulk of the carcass. Nothing else stirred. Just the little jackal, one of the smallest of the carrion beasts, and the immense meal. The visitors watched in horrified amusement as the small animal began to feed, its head twitching in anxiety as it glanced around, waiting for the greater scavengers to arrive. One jackal with an entire elephant to itself!

Their guide smiled. He said, "Archbishop Tutu once said that the only way to eat an elephant is one bite at a time!"

One bite at a time! That perfectly reflects the journeyman's philosophy I have been learning throughout my lifetime. The "elephant of negativity" will only disappear if we eat it. If we eat it, it will make us strong and positive in our outlook. The only way to eat it is the way of the jackal—one bite at a time!

The Menu at the Elephant Restaurant

I do not intend to weigh you down with theory! Here are the key principles of my positivity hack. You do not need to memorize them or figure out how to put them into action. If you come back to them later, you will see exactly how they have fallen into place. Some people like to know what lies ahead, however, and as you face the "elephant," here is what you can expect:

- **The principle of atomization:** large projects can be best achieved by small steps. Moving out of negativity into positivity does not require impossible goals, but can "only" be achieved by very small achievements.
- **The principle of patience**: You can take as long as you like. This is your life and you are in charge. You must, however, be patient with yourself, and shake off any outside pressure to make instant dramatic changes. I am not perfectly positive, but I am more and more positive every year.
- **Understanding your own weakness**: Some people fear that admitting to weakness is giving in to negativity. However, noticing that you tend to have a negative mindset is the only way to escape it!

- **Understanding your own strength**: You will be pleasantly surprised to find how strong you are in being able to take the path of atomic steps! Ordinary people have an extraordinary capacity and unrealized potential to emerge into positivity.
- **Evaluating past failures:** When you are lying awake at night tormented by your mistakes and their consequences, your fears and their threats, or your hurts and your anger, it seems difficult to "let go" of the past. My little way of atomic steps will show you how to stop allowing them to consume you. There is a difference between "evaluation" and "dwelling on."

YIN AND YANG: CLOSED CIRCLE OR UPWARDS SPIRAL?

Negative and Positive coexist. The negative shows your positive side that you might not realize, or perhaps it shows that you are covering up the positive. The positive shows your negative side, reminding you of your dark side. Beware of it. The negative is here, but the positive has invisible powers to stop it from harming you.

There are an infinite number of ways of applying yin-yang philosophy to life. Opposing forces in balance (or out of balance) can describe every aspect of our existence. Tension between positive and negative forces in our "live scan" must be balanced in three ways. The negative can statically balance the positive, leaving us motionless. This is not what the yin-yang philosophy intends, but like all philosophies, people can sometimes misapply the logic. We have seen, however, that the negative always strives to increase. A second mistaken balance can be found in allowing the negative to constantly swallow the positive, leaving us in a downward vortex.

My understanding is that the positive energy of the yang in our lives receives and consumes the negative yin. Yang protects us from the Yin. The net result is a rising spiral of positivity. The approach of "my little way of atomic steps" is based on the expectation that we can indeed achieve "a constant, *dynamic* balance of all things" in an upward spiral (Wang, 2022).

Now that we have established—on "Monday"—how difficult our life situations can become, we need to chart a course for our journey into a positive mindset. Chapter 2 introduces us to fainting goats and their surprising lessons on how to break the spell cast by negativity in our lives!

SUMMARY

- Every human being experiences significant negativity.
- The experience of being overwhelmed by negativity can lead to paralysis.
- Negativity infects our existence and makes us uncomfortable.
- It causes physical, emotional, social, and spiritual damage.
- Negativity never gets better by itself—it only gets worse.
- Anyone, however, has the capacity to escape negativity.
- The way to overcome paralysis is by planning small steps.
- We need to find a life-giving balance between the negative and the positive in our life.

CHAPTER 2
ATOMIC STEPS ON A PATH OF DESIRE

INSIGHT FROM A CAR BREAKDOWN

Imagine that you hire a car on a snowy day. You pick up the keys, load your bags in the trunk, and cautiously pull out of the car-park. You now face a lengthy cross-country journey on icy roads to a little town in the mountains, where you are scheduled to lead a team-building conference featuring a cross-country hike to a distant cabin.

Everything goes well. You head out into the countryside, the windscreen wipers easily coping with the light sleet blowing onto your windscreen. On either side, the woods draw in until you are driving between walls of dark trees on either side. The sunsets, and the light is gone.

And then the engine cuts out!

You coast to the edge of the road and try to restart. Nothing. Something has gone catastrophically wrong with the electrics, and you are stranded in the dark, in the snow, and in the woods. Do you have a strategy for this scenario?

Do you wait in the car for some random stranger to stop? Have you put out your hazard triangles? Have you turned on your hazard lights? Sadly, these will soon drain your battery, so your car will be vulnerable to two threats—some other vehicle colliding with it in the dark or somebody wanting to either rob you or con you.

If you do not want to be a victim of a roadside crime or be involved in a secondary accident, one law firm recommends this course of action—put on all the heavy hiking gear you came with and set out the hazard triangles you should have in your trunk. Then walk away and settle down in the dark, where you can still see your car without being seen yourself (Hastings & Hastings, 2014). Anyone who is not well-intentioned will not be able to see you while you wait for the assistance you have called in. If another vehicle collides with yours, you will not be injured.

Everyone does situation-simulation planning—commercial, military, sporting, educational, or whatever. Preparing tactics for different possible scenarios is an effective way to stay safe, have success, and be positive.

You are reading this because your life feels like it has broken down. This book is my tactical approach of learning to cope with the negativity breakdown. We will run through some scenarios and get ready to move from where we are to the place we want to be.

The question is: Where *do* we want to be? What is your "place of positivity"? How will we recognize it once we get there? And what steps can we take to get there?

TRAPPED IN "THINK" MODE

One problem, if you're like me, is that your car has already broken down before you think about the possibility. You realize that you are trapped in negativity once it has already happened. It's not too late to figure out a good way ahead, but human beings are prone to function on instinct in a crisis, and instinct is not always a reliable guide.

Our human response to a threat is to do one of three things—fight, flee, or freeze (Legg & Gepp, 2020). There are three ways that reacting to negativity on pure instinct can go wrong. The first is that we lash out in fight mode, perhaps hurting others or ourselves. Like a hiker in quicksand, our intense reactions draw us deeper into negativity. The second instinctual way is to flee, but we do it all wrong. We try to escape through drugs or alcohol. Some of us try to escape into longer hours and harder work. Some people resign on a whim and then find themselves jobless and in deeper negativity. The most common reaction to negativity, however, is option number three—freezing. We are thinking up a storm, but we cannot do what we need to do.

Insight From Fainting Goats

Have you come across fainting goats? These animals (officially known as myotonic goats) freeze and fall over if you give them too much of a shock. It looks hilarious, but it seems that it is not a trait that would ensure the survival of their species! (Gibbens, 2017) Are you a fainting goat? I have been exactly here in the place of paralysis. You are longing to not be irritable, jealous, sad, afraid, or negative. Day by day, though, you continue to feel sad, shocked, angry, disgusted, and afraid. You are overthinking until your thoughts drive you crazy, but you are not able to get moving out of your negative mindset.

The ancient Greeks worshiped a deity they called Pan, who at times caused people to react with sudden surges of fear and terror. The Greeks were recognizing and describing the inexplicable and mysterious forces that caused irrational reactions, which we still call "panic." And often, that irrational reaction is to freeze, a condition that has been around since the dawn of time. You are not the first person to find themselves paralyzed by negativity.

However, you are not a goat. You might become the GOAT in some area of your life, though, if you can figure out how to get moving towards positivity. Whether or not some hostile spiritual entity wants you to fail and quail is a discussion for a religious forum. In the meantime, I am here to give you a friendly message. You might be surprised to know that *you have already taken* the first step on that journey.

LONGING FOR ESCAPE

The longing to be free is the first step to getting yourself free.

Insight From an Elephant's Chain

Asian elephants are astonishingly powerful animals. Usually tourists encounter them as friendly, ambling giants, happy to take you for a ride, and always scrounging fruit or vegetables. However, once they are put to work in the jungles of Thailand, you see that their huge bodies are heavily muscled. Their trunks can lift huge logs and boulders. You cannot build a fence strong enough to keep wild elephants out of your banana plantation.

Yet domesticated elephants are kept in place by a chain that they could snap with a slight jerk. So, why does a chain work to keep control of an elephant? The answer is conditioning. Little elephants get chained as soon as they are born. I don't like the thought of it, but that is what happens. When they are tiny, they cannot break the chain, so they learn to ignore the potential for escape. This habit of mind stays with the elephant as it grows. Slowly it matures to become a full-grown animal, but every night the chain goes back on. The elephant is now more than strong enough to break free, but it does not.

So, are you a chained elephant who is beginning to long for freedom? You have become used to negative thinking since childhood. Do you realize just how powerful you have become, though? Or is that one of the negative links in that chain—a nagging sense of self deprecation? If you are discontent with the negativity to such an extent that you are following me on this exploration, you have outmuscled the chain of negativity, and it only takes one broken link to be free. Your discontent already shows that you *believe in the possibility* of a positive life already. You are chafing at that chain. Let's snap it and walk away!

THE PRINCIPLE OF VISUALIZATION

One key principle for good outcomes, as we explored while reflecting on car breakdown dynamics, is to visualize them and choose one that suits you. You are not doomed to failure and life-long capture! NO! If you calmly turn your attention to your predicament, you can figure a way out, for sure. Human beings can think imaginatively, and our imagination can draw us pictures of happiness ahead. We will discuss this process in detail later in our "Monday" chapter, but I need to prime the pump a little first.

Visualizing What You Want to Break Free From

I get a huge amount of control over negativity if I first *visualize* and specifically *name* what I intend to get free from (Ames, 2022). I don't say, "I'm upset." That simply means, "I am out of equilibrium." I say, "I don't understand why my supplier in Italy did not tell me there was a delay in receiving the accessories, which caused a severe delay in production," or "I am afraid because I think I messed up on one question in my exam, and I think I might fail the course." Haul those negative feelings and situations out into the sunlight.

Visualizing What You Want Your Life to Look Like

I cement my control over negativity by visualizing the positive outcomes. I am very specific. "I am glad that my Italian supplier will learn from the fallout and feedback, and that all my future orders will be filled smoothly and on time," or "I remember how easily I answered all the other questions. Although I might not get an "A+," I will easily pass this exam and be able to go on successfully with my studies."

All you need is the "desire to desire." You have shown that you want to move towards a positive mindset by opening this book. A positive future is opening up to you, and you can decide what it looks like. I will be applauding every step you take. Consider me your cheerleader!

The Principle of Intention: Why You Never Get What You Do Not Desire

"If you aim at nothing, you will get exactly what you aim at." Yeah, sure, it's an old cliche, but it still packs a punch. In a thousand years, we will be able to find it in "Words of Wisdom from the Ancient Business World," which will be on bookshelves in retro bookstores alongside Sun Tzu's "Art of War." The truth is that if you do not want something specific, you are unlikely to get it.

Insight From a Letter to Santa

Think of it as a letter to Santa Claus:

"Dear Santa," writes the first child, "Can I please have the video game Jumanji?"

"Ho, ho!" laughs Santa and shouts to the packing elves, "Load a Jumanji for this kid!"

The second child writes, "Dear Santa. I hope you are well. I would love to get a 'Designafriend Rosie Doll' for Christmas, unless you are too busy."

"Ho, ho!" chuckles Santa and shouts to the packing elves, "Gift wrap a Rosie Doll for this one!"

The next child writes, "Dear Santa, I'm unhappy with the toys I have. The dog chewed them."

No laughs from Santa. He pauses and strokes his beard. Then he shouts off to the research elf, "Here's another kid who doesn't know what he wants!"

Next time you think about the dimensions of your personal future, remember how you used to let Santa Claus know what you wanted! Be innocent—be simple and straightforward—and ask from your heart, not your brain. Or, to return to another childhood memory, remember how the Genie said to Aladdin, "My master, your wish is my command." Aladdin had to make specific wishes, and they had to be exactly what he wanted because he got exactly what he asked for! You simply receive what you wish for. Adults forget valuable lessons they learned as children once they become too rational. Santa Claus and Aladdin are important parables about clearly visualized intentions!

Do you know what you would like if you could get it? Visualize it and write it down.

- Peaceful sleep at night?
- Friendly relationships at work?
- Respect from your children?
- A degree from your favorite university?
- Assignment to a more interesting work stream?
- No more feelings of choking anger?
- Complete confidence in social situations?

I take this very seriously for myself. I record my visualizations in a "dream book." I keep it under my pillow; my hand can touch it from time to time as I stir in my sleep, and I feel soothed and comforted. Sometimes, I wake up in the morning with clarity about what I really want in a situation. I suggest that you regularly record your "dream notes." Even if I have no great revelation, I feel reassured knowing that I won't miss out on anything important that drifts through my subconscious. You could simply start with a sheet of paper for tomorrow morning. Even though the obstacles or issues might still remain, writing down your positive visualizations achieves at least one of your goals—peaceful sleep!

Recently, I have been too active and exhausted to wake up much at night, but if I do stir, I enjoy this half-sleeping-half-awake moment.

It's one of the best times to practice the visualizations and self-affir-mations that I have recorded in my dream book! It works really well for me. If *you* struggle to sleep because of some sort of inner turmoil, don't switch on the light and write! Rather, use the wakeful time to recall and repeat your positive affirmations or focus on your most important visualizations. In the dark and quiet, you can visu-alize your desires, your happiness, and your tomorrow. Instead of overthinking at this half-awake stage, think about all the kindnesses you have received, your passionate interests, or do some self-affirma-tion. Embrace your pillow as if you are holding your positive dreams, and doze off into deep sleep.

Visualization works! The actor Will Smith said, "In my mind, I've always been an A-list Hollywood superstar. Y'all just didn't know yet" (Ames, 2022).

THE PERSPECTIVE OF A WHOLE LIFE AHEAD

A change of perspective can jolt us out of panic and paralysis. Our panic tells us that we are stuck in negativity, and we want out *immedi-ately*. But nothing has changed since yesterday, panic notices! I am doomed to be stuck in this negativity forever, says panic!

Impatience causes desire to backfire. The backlash comes immedi-ately. If things have not improved dramatically in a few days, we feel like we have failed again. That's like buying shares today on the stock market, selling them tomorrow, and wondering why you've made a loss. Compound interest, that magical mathematical force, needs *time* to turn your investment into millions!

However, the immediate pain and darkness remain, and out of respect for your genuine desire to move away from pain towards healing, let me introduce you to another positivity hack of mine.

Get perspective.

Insight From Bear Grylls

Bear Grylls, the famous adventurer, points out that gaining a view-point on the whole of your problem is essential for survival and rescue in the wild (Grylls, 2013). If you are lost, get up high enough to see how the land lies, he says. You will see how the mountains lie and how the rivers run. Heck, you might even see a farmhouse or nearby village!

If you are chafing and impatient about your situation, the first thing to do is take stock of where exactly you are. Take a few deep breaths. Then look for a place of perspective. The landscape you need to evaluate is the rest of your life.

In order to gain this sense of perspective, I slowly drink a glass of water—simple, room-temperature water. I imagine its healing energy flowing into my body as I slowly drink it. I thank the water, and I tell myself, "I'm drinking in positive energy with this water. Later, it will leave my system, taking with it all my negativity." This is a useful atomic step, and by attaching my mood to the simple rhythms of my body, I find that positivity automatically rises in my consciousness.

You are not limited. You have a full life to live. Furthermore, you might have faced serious adversity so far, but imagine yourself looking back on yourself ten years from now. You might be just about to make it out of the shadows. How you get perspective is the subject of Part 2 of this book, where I lay out the seven-day process of moving from negative to positive. We get perspective by looking backwards, forwards, inwards, and outwards. That perspective shows us something about the desires that should be pulling us forward to snap that leg chain, but puzzlingly, they're not.

JUST WANTING SOMETHING CAN GO BADLY WRONG

Insight from Sourdough: A Loaf of Possibilities!

There are three options for desire: Disappointment, despair, or hope.

As I have tried to explain, desire without patience can tumble you back deeper into negativity. During Covid-19 lockdowns, there was a craze for making sourdough bread. Everybody seemed to become an expert baker, and social media was full of pictures of delicious-looking loaves of bread (although nobody posted pictures of their flops and failures!). The quest for the perfect sourdough loaf illustrates the three potential outcomes of our desire for positivity.

Firstly, you have to harness the power of the wild yeast that floats around everywhere in the atmosphere. You mix flour and water and keep it at room temperature for five days or so to start bubbling, pouring off some of the yeast mixture and adding new flour and water every day (Christensen, 2020). This is the start of the starter that you will use continually in the future. In these first five days, some people will be disappointed with their results. Some will despair and stop being bakers. Some, however, will continue in hope. Those who continue in hope, hungry enough for their own sourdough bread, realize that their starter will only get better over time. Positivity, like yeast, comes from many sources around us and within us, but it needs hope to bubble up!

Disappointment and despair can snuff out our dream for sourdough success at many more points, though. When your starter is ready, you take a spoonful of the bubbly mix and mix it with a small amount of flour and water to make the leaven for the loaf. Leave it overnight, and you'll find that it's bubbling and popping with micro-bial vigor the next day. You are ready to make a loaf of bread! If disappointment and despair hog-tie you and you do not do this, then there is no hope for you. You will have to make do with bread from the deli.

But you have hope! Not certainty, not confidence, not super-affirmative positivity yet, but hope! Hope is the delicate bubbling leaven that will grow with enough power to supercharge your mighty and glorious bread. Positivity does not flood your life from the outside and sweep everything negative away. It invades, infects, and expands in your life from the first signs of bubbling yeast!

Don't expect your life to look completely positive immediately. The atomic step theory requires fermentation first, and fermentation is not pretty! During the bubbling process, the leaven looks disgusting and smells rather weird. It's slimy to the touch! But this is a process that leads you to deep satisfaction later.

Then you add the leaven to the bread and water, which will be your final golden-brown product. You mix it in, knead it up, and let it rest for a few hours. Enzymes do their magic, carbohydrates break down into sugars, and hope rises! You add some salt, knead, and fold the dough to make the gluten stretch and grow into a springy dough that fights back when you punch it! And then you let it rest again for half an hour while it bulks out like a body-builder on steroids! Disappointment and despair never got this far, but hopeful visualization has almost brought you to the oven!

In it goes! The heat performs its miracles of caramelization and crisping—and out comes the perfect, fragrant loaf of positivity! Well done, patient baker! Take a photo for Instagram and grab a slice quickly before your family and friends polish it off and demand more!

Desire can go badly wrong, but it can also go magnificently right!

Insight From a Mechanical Hand

Positive desires often need negative desires.

Some people think that it is childish and irrational to be happy all the time and never pay attention to the negative aspects of life. That is so wrong. Positivity is the tough-minded capacity to not let negative realities *control* your reading of the future. Positivity is actually robustly negative—to negativity!

This is not just playing with words. In 2019, engineer Ian Davis lost all four fingers on his left hand in a gruesome work accident (Sheth, 2021). The pain and shock of such a loss were a huge negative blow. It was made infinitely more negative by his insurance company pointing out that since he had only lost his fingers and not his whole hand, they were not obliged to pay him any compensation. This sort of legal fancy footwork has often threatened my positive outlook on life, too. Commercially available prostheses are expensive and slow-moving. An engineer needs to be able to pick up a spanner immediately when he needs it, and not have to wait two seconds for an electric motor to close his fingers. Plus, manufacturers of prosthetic hands don't allow you to make your own repairs and improvements. You are locked into their design and repair regimes.

Anyway, Davis had some hefty challenges. He could not "positive away" his lost fingers. He could not "positively ignore" his insurance company's unhelpfulness. He could not "positively wave away" the red-tape of commercial options. So, he did what any learner of positivity needs to do. He nixed the negativities in his life with some hard-hitting, practical positivity.

He went into his workshop and started designing his own mechanical left-hand prosthesis from scratch. The results have been remarkable. Davis has created a powerful mechanical hand that allows him to work at full potential. His iron-man digits can bend individually, splay, grip, or extend with gear-whirring efficiency. Using steel and brass fittings that he has fitted and turned himself, as well as miniature industrial chains, springs, leather, and straps, he has produced a feisty, steam-punk solution that allows him to show any finger or combination of fingers he likes to his insurance company!

Not everyone has the *skills* of an Ian Davis. But anyone can develop his *attitude*. The man knows that a positive attitude does not weakly wish things had not happened. He knows that he does not have to pity himself for his misfortunes. That is the gritty basis of positivity that is available to every human being on this planet. He has found the right target for his negative feelings. All of his anger, disgust, fear, shock, and grief have been turned into a plasma torch that cuts through the negative circumstances he finds himself in. Imagine—visualize—what you could achieve if you turned all those negative feelings you have about yourself into tools for changing your circumstances!

ACHIEVING A POSITIVE MINDSET AS AN ORDINARY PERSON

This is ultra-important! I, myself, am not a guru. You do not need to be a guru to benefit from some of their insights. What I live by is not some hard-to-attain, elaborate mystical construct. The path of atomic steps is a simple and straightforward approach to life.

So many of my insights have come to me during the enforced leisure time of international flights. It occurred to me recently, on a flight into La Guardia, that I did not know how to fly an airplane. That's not a big deal, you might say. Not many people can! What I realized, however, was that although I could not fly an airplane, I could nonetheless fly! I did not have to be able to handle the controls to be able to travel long distances at the same time as the pilot. In the same way, in my quest to escaping negativity and seek positivity. I have depended on insights from the experts. Ordinary people can do extraordinary things without having to first morph into superhuman! The way of atomic steps is within the capacity of any human being!

ONE WEEK AWAY FROM A POSITIVE MINDSET!

A single week in a year can be the pivot on which your company goes from "red" into "black," or your sports team goes from the chasing pack to the top of the log. In the science of positivity, it seems to me that one week is the molecule of positivity (yes, I do know positives cancel negatives in a molecule—this is just an illustration!) and the seven days are the atoms of change!

I could have used some other metaphor or even an Excel spreadsheet to make my point. Ignatius of Loyola used the concept of "four weeks in a month" to express a similar objective (Ignatian Spirituality, 2022). It seems to me, though, that a "week of seven days" is the best way to explain my little theory of atomic steps.

Everyone experiences time as a flow of days and weeks. Days are short, but significant enough to carry 86,400 seconds, themselves each a potential vehicle for an atomic step. If you miss one second, you do not have to worry. You still have the whole day ahead of you. Days have space for resting and eating, sleeping and working, playing and thinking. A day is not a frightening or intimidating concept. The day will pass, but tomorrow will give you another one. On one hand, it's short and simple. On the other hand, a day is long enough to live and breathe. My "atomic steps approach" to escape negativity envisions just one of those seconds in that leisurely day devoted to a small step towards positivity.

Those ordinary, unspectacular days are themselves embedded in an ordinary week. Weeks come and go. They take us forward to the future gently and without fuss. All humanity orders their lives by this undemanding schedule. Humans do indeed stress up their weeks and days, but days in themselves are rhythmic and predictable, with space for all we need as well as the occasional spark of creativity and change. The pivotal weeks of our existence do not arrive by leapfrogging the rest of the calendar. They turn up in their course, on the back of old weeks and as foundations for the next.

Peaceful, revolutionary change happens with tiny achievements and small demands. I always say to myself (and everyone else)—we are driving ourselves too hard, and it's causing tension. Step back, hold on a bit, and we will be able to see what is happening with more clarity of perspective.

One aspect of perspective is that you've got all the time you need. It is not your fault that you are hemmed in by negativity, any more than it was the engineer's fault that he lost his fingers. However, the way out is *not* going to demand more strength than you already have, hard as that might seem to you now.

Another aspect of perspective is that "perfection" can also drag you down. If you are too obsessive about the appearance of your experimental prosthesis, you might never start using your iron hand in the workshop. Don't let a quest for perfection paralyze or diminish your peaceful progress through life. A true lifetime perspective will show you that nothing you can do will be perfect—but that your "imperfect" achievements can also be truly remarkable!

You Are in Charge of Your "Week"

My experience is that these seemingly insignificant steps have kept me ahead of negativity and moving towards positivity all my life. It's not a spectacular process, but it works. The steps are tiny and painless, free from stress and outside expectations. You do not need to have the leisure of the super-wealthy to follow this process. You can be completely immersed in studies, labor, or commerce and not find that they interfere with your time or your focus on your goals. You might be collecting recyclables from a trash dump in a city where you are a refugee—these atomic steps will have the same powerful effect on your life.

Of course, as a businessman, I expect you to undertake a cost-benefit analysis of the process. Please do. You will find that the investment is tiny, but following the atomic seven-step journey out of negativity yields lifelong positive benefits.

Come with me on a relaxing tour of a "week" of small daily initiatives and insights that will end at the place you so badly want to be —having a positive mindset. We start with "Monday," and reflect more deeply on the art of visualization.

SUMMARY

- We can get where we want to be if we can visualize where it is.
- We have lots of time to get into a positive mindset—our whole lives.
- Hope is a positive guide through disappointment and defeat.
- Ordinary people can become positive using their ordinary abilities.

The "week of atomic steps" can be longer or shorter, regular or occasional.

PART TWO
A WEEK OF SMALL STEPS

Imagine a different sort of Monday morning! Allow me to introduce you to a Monday worth waking up to!

My week of atomic steps is a simple, seven-day approach to taking the smallest of steps, repeatedly, that will ease you out of negativity and into a positive mindset. There is a whole week lying ahead of you, stretching out in a restful path of seven stepping stones. Monday is the day to put your strategy for the week in order. Let us set out on a seven-day week in which we find an inner balance to our world. In my life, each day has its own atomic step to take and its own daily insights in moving towards Sunday and even next Monday, which will be more positive than this one!

MONDAY: ATTRACTION— CALLING IN THE POSITIVE

Let's start at the beginning of the week and enjoy a different way of living through the week!

Are you living in fear? This Monday might find you extremely anxious, and, ironically, you might be the cause of your own stress. "Imposter syndrome" is the struggle many people have when they feel that they do not *deserve* to have achieved their success or their promotion. Fear gnaws away at their consciousness—anxiety that someone will "find them out" and "expose them as imposters" (Weir, 2013).

This is not based on the truth! You are the genuine article, and you have gotten to where you are through hard work and expertise! The most likely scenario is that you are a high-achieving individual with plenty more potential. You not only deserve your success, but you deserve more!

Negative effects can be harbingers of healing and positivity. We just need to look at them the right way!

First, are you starting your week with *negative* visualization? Are you dreading meeting your supervisor, your boss, or your branch manager? Are you having to deal with complaints about last week? Well, if you have to, you have to. But you *can* change something— your visualization of how the negative encounters can go the right way! You can visualize yourself harnessing those challenges to achieve a positive outcome.

It's like being sick. When I have been running a temperature, healing from the flu, I roll myself up in a sheet. This is like being in the grip of a negative mindset. The breakthrough comes when I start to perspire profusely. Sure, I get disgusting and stinky, which seems like a negative effect! The virus is receding quietly, though, and the sweating is a sign that my white blood cells have won the battle! This Monday is when we start forming the immunity of posi- tivity, as your positive white blood cells deal with the virus of nega- tivity and build up a long-lasting immune defense.

So, what sort of negativity is making you feel less-than-well today?

- Are you imagining not reaching a deadline and getting into trouble?
- Are you afraid that your intimate partner is not as loving as they were, and are you wondering how you can make yourself more attractive?
- Are you concerned that you are going to run out of money before the end of the month, and you are imagining going hungry?

Anything like this beckons you onward on the "Monday" of the journey of small steps. Monday is the day we change the way we visualize the future!

The way to move ahead happily and peacefully in life is to start your week with "Attraction"—consciously calling the positive outcomes you deserve and long for. Monday, as the first day of the week, is the appropriate day on which to embed this primary strategic element, which will make the entire mood of the week lighter, more hopeful, and more effective. The key technique for doing this (taking one atomic step at a time!) is called "visualization."

Give it a try. Don't see yourself losing. Think, *I can win!*

As you continue to read, you'll find the following "days," especially Saturday and Sunday, will prime your Monday for more positivity in turn—next Monday, your positive visualizations will be a little easier! It's a positive cycle of changing your negativity to positivity! We just had to start somewhere.

Imagine this: Edward and Sean know that the office will be downsizing and letting staff go this week. The company is also restructuring at a regional level, so there will be some openings for promotion. Edward imagines the worst! He visualizes getting fired and having to look for a new job. As a result, he looks so unhappy and has such a lack of energy at work that he does indeed get fired! Sean visualizes getting a promotion. He is so full of positive energy and creative ideas that he catches the eye of management, and they offer him one of the vacancies at the regional office. Edward and Sean have different visions of the future. Both are accurate visualizations. I just wish that Edward had a better way of looking ahead!

THE SCIENCE OF VISUALIZATION (ALSO KNOWN AS "ATTRACTION")

If, like me, you love reading about the science of positivity, your first reaction might be, "Again? Visualization? Really?" Give me a chance. I guarantee that my approach is different!

To delve deep into the dynamics of visualization, let's take a sudden 5000-year jolt backwards in time.

Insight From San Rock Art

New evidence shows that the San peoples of the Kalahari (formerly called "bushmen") first painted their vibrant rock art more than 5000 years ago (Geggel, 2017). They painted anatomically correct kudu and eland, and the circles of hunters (also anatomically correct!) One thing all the paleontologists agree on in their interpretative theories is that these wise and passionate hunters were painting for themselves—not for spectators. Whether they visualized successful hunting or whether they used the paintings to train new hunters, or to appeal to God to lead them to their prey, they were creative visualizations, examples of imagining specific positive outcomes.

Being a successful human has *always* needed the ability to visualize what is not yet there!

Hana Ames, researcher for Dr. Robert Kilitz, records that positive visualization sets the "creative potential of your subconscious" in action and allows you to develop "creative ideas for achieving your goals." Visualization alerts you to what you need, and when you need it in order to get that positive outcome. It also helps you stay motivated to take any small steps you need to keep taking! (Ames, 2022)

These are the neurological realities that kick in whenever humans pray or meditate. You do not have to be a hyper-disciplined spiritual practitioner to take atomic steps—your brain is pre-programmed to take them! Whenever you calmly reflect on the positive future rather than the negative future, the beautifully flexible neural network in your brain opens up surprisingly effective new ways of looking at your life.

There are two issues that need to be dealt with through visualization. The first is tackling the world *outside* you when it only seems to offer a dead-end future of failure. The other is tackling that *inner* world where you are so strangely negative about yourself. I am committed to the process of Care—Think—Act, and visualization has a powerful motivating effect in all those areas.

ATTRACTING A TRANSFORMED OUTER WORLD—CHANGING YOUR POINT OF VIEW

I do not know what challenges your world is bringing to you. Are you afraid that people are plotting against you? Are you having to live life without a limb? Do you not have enough resources to get the education you want? Does your line boss not think your value to the company merits a raise? The possibilities are endless, and I do NOT want to go further down that road. You do not have to go further down that road either!

Insight From the Film Industry

In the world of film-making, the point of view of the camera is crucial to telling the story. Scriptwriters and camera personnel have their own acronym for it, which everyone in the business knows as: Point of view (POV)! If you want to make something seem important to your viewers, bring the cameras in close and low. The POV makes the person, building, or machine look big and threatening, looming above the viewer. If, on the other hand, the producer wants to make something seem small and insignificant, then he sends up a drone, and the POV of the camera is high above the person, building, or machine, making it feel unimportant in comparison to the wide sweep of the countryside (Studiobinder, 2021).

The thing itself remains the same but the POV controls its power. Visualization is literally a change in the POV you take of your difficulties—and your goals.

Experts in the theory of attraction explain that there are three components to this way of seeing reality—like attracts like, nature abhors a vacuum, and the present is always perfect. (Regan, 2021)

Like Attracts Like

When we approach life from an inner negative point of view, we attract and collect negative events, people, relationships, and life-story tangents. It's not magic. We fit better with the negative, and the negative fits better with us. Toxic relationships and disastrous outcomes haunt us in our imaginations and then in reality. We see the negative elements looming over us because we are down on the ground looking up at life.

On the other hand, if like attracts like, then approaching life from a positive POV means positive people, relationships, events, and life-story tangents can "see us and find us." Our positive energy resonates with the positive.

Two people are experiencing exactly the same difficulties. The one is crushed. The other thrives. The difference is in the attractive power of their *point of view*.

Like Attracts Like—Atomic Steps

- Think of your happiest moment from last week.
- What would you like to match it in the coming week?
- Think of that happening in a good way.
- Don't worry if your visualization seems unrealistic. Make it Big! Visualize the most excellent outcome! When it comes to picturing your best future, the sky's the limit!

Vacuums Always Fill Up

The Greek philosopher Aristotle (384–322 BC) first proposed that "nature abhors a vacuum." If my life is full of negative energy, I can't expect positive energy to flow into it. But if I empty out some negative attitudes and expectations, I create an "attitude-vacuum," and encouraging and exciting positive options can then have an opportunity to get drawn into me.

It is strange but true that many people live by the proverb "better the devil you know than the one you don't." They feel secure in the negative world they have learned to cope with, and they worry that any changes might make things worse. Yes, things could perhaps get worse. If your POV is that there are only devils out there, however, you are never going to notice all those angels queuing up with positive energy. A change in your POV is very likely to lead you to unexpected pleasure and positivity.

Vacuums Fill Themselves—Atomic Steps

- What have you noticed that is missing in your life?
- What would you like to be sucked into your life in its place?
- Visualize one positive thing you would like to start noticing in your life

The Perfect Present

This is a preparedness to look beyond the negative present to a positive future. We "perfect the present moment" when we discern that whatever it is that distresses us has brought us to a point where we can leave it behind. We don't say that terrible things are "perfect;" what we do is bring the distress to its perfect conclusion, and find that in the dynamics of yin and yang we can launch from the present moment into a brighter future. "Toxic positivity" is what we call declaring that something distressing is "not distressing"— untruth always poisons us. Perfecting the present means that we treat our current difficulties as a step to elevate us rather than a burden to crush us.

There will always be enough things around to make us unhappy if we focus on them—especially things we lack. If we focus instead on things we deeply desire, we shift our reality.

The Perfect Present—Atomic Steps

- Imagine you are starting your life over from today.
- What would you like to happen to you?
- Visualize a positive future in as many ways that you can

Insight From an Escapee

Megan Lundstrom offers us a moving glimpse into how positive visualization helped her escape the men who trafficked her for prostitution. At 23, Lundstrom was drawn into the world of sex-for-hire through the violent manipulation of her first "boyfriend." Eventually, he sold her on to another pimp, and Lundstrom's life was spiraling down to a disastrous end, earning $1,000 a day for her pimp and getting nothing but abuse in return.

Her outward circumstances remained exactly the same, but she describes how her inner point of view shifted. It started with her imagining spending more time with her children. Soon, that was what she was doing. Then she imagined going home to her father. It wasn't long before she did. After that, she developed a longing to study. The next thing she knew, she had earned an undergraduate degree in finance. It is interesting to notice how Lunstrom's goals emerged organically out of her negative experience. Without coaching, she discovered how to "perfect the moment" and escape the negative spiral. Her ability to imagine a slightly different world enabled her to break the chains of manipulation and abuse. The power to change came from within.

Lundstrom went on to become an expert in her field, and now she runs an Instagram account that has helped many other trafficked women visualize and achieve a different outcome to their lives. (Tucker, 2021)

ATTRACTING A TRANSFORMED INNER WORLD —THE WITNESSES FOR YOUR DEFENSE

Warning: Courtroom drama! In this segment, I am about to take a very different approach to visualization that will push your imagination to the limits! It's going to be fun!

You know the old saying, "Sticks and stones may break my bones, but names will never harm me," right?

Wrong. That is a flat-out lie!

At times, my mind has been a courtroom ringing with hurtful accusations and false evidence. They have all called me nasty, mean-spirited names: "Lazy;" "unqualified;" "unmotivated;" "unattractive;" "unsuccessful;" and many more. I have sat as the lone juror in the case against myself, and I have condemned myself to be every negative thing that people have told me. I have been shaped by the ill-wishes of others.

Worse than that, I myself have been a witness for the prosecution. I have told the court really bad things about myself. I have knocked my skills and mocked my own capacities. I have exaggerated my flaws and minimized my strengths to almost nothing.

I have also been the judge. I have been my own judge and condemned myself to the prison of dark negativity.

Let us bring a firm close to this state of affairs by taking an atomic step away from it. Imagine that you are accused of all sorts of negative things by others (and yourself). Let's imagine (visualize) that you are in a courtroom. Let's give all this negative condemnation a retrial! On Monday, let's call in the witnesses for the defense, and overturn the old verdict with a positive one! We are calling in the positive and attracting a better outcome.

Visualize Clarity and Attract Positivity—Witness 1: Your Illusion Buster Self

The first witness is a straight-talking, no bullshit version of yourself. This is your Illusion Buster Self, and you stalk up to the witness stand as if you own the room, brimming with confidence.

"The witnesses say the accused is really awful," says the lawyer. "What is your response?"

"It's a load of crap!" you say. If you don't usually swear, give it a try. Swearing is scientifically proven to help you tough out bad situations. (Mohiyeddini & Beaumont, 2020) "None of it is true! This person is kind and attractive! They're intelligent, sensitive, courageous, and committed. This is one of the best people in the world!"

"But," the lawyer prods, "the accused says the same bad things about themselves."

"Well, I call bullshit!", the Illusion Buster Self barks. "They have been holding my friend captive. My friend is only agreeing so they will stop the torture."

Turning to face you directly, Illusion Buster Self looks you right in the eyes. "You're way better than what these jerks are saying about you, aren't you!

"Yes," you say in a weak voice.

Illusion Buster Self persists: "You understand that they have been keeping you under a cloud of criticism, don't you!"

"Yes," you say in a firmer voice. You are suddenly feeling more cheerful.

Illusion Buster Self drives home his point: "You don't believe all these lies anymore, do you!" he shouts.

"No!" you shout back. "I am creative and thoughtful, intelligent, and kind! I am generous and responsible, and I am attractive and interesting!" The crowd in the gallery cheers! The prosecution lawyer scowls. The judge hides a smile behind her hand. Things are looking good for you in this retrial.

Reflections for your Illusion Buster Self

Say one truthful, positive thing about your good qualities to yourself all day today. This is an atomic step towards positivity!

Some examples of Visualization

- I'm A-Class
- I'm qualified
- I'm motivated
- I'm attractive
- I'm the best

Visualize Clarity and Attract Positivity—Witness 2: Your Skilled Self

The next witness is you again, dressed for doing the things you do best. Power dressed if you are an executive. Or wearing a crisply ironed overall and welding gloves. These are real skills you have. Your Skilled Self steps up to the witness stand and glares at your accusers.

The prosecution lawyer begins: "All the witnesses say that the accused can't do their job properly. What do you say?"

"I have a degree in business science." your Skilled Self says. Or perhaps, "I can weld a seam perfectly. If you were a seam-welder, there would be more Titanics on the seabed! Where is your evidence I can't do my job? All my work assessments are very positive."

"No more questions for this witness." says the lawyer quickly. This is going badly for the case for continued negativity. Deep in your heart, you know that what Your Skilled Self is saying is the truth about you.

If you have a stressful meeting on your calendar, write something like "I'm unbeatable. I'm invincible. I'm intelligent. I'm the world. I'm Abundance."

- You do know stuff.
- You are not an imposter.
- You deserve to be where you are and do what you do.
- No amount of mockery or dismissive negativity or self-sabotage can *take away* your abilities.

Reflections on Your Skills

Tell yourself one truthful, positive thing about your skills. Write it on your bathroom mirror or tie a tag with it onto the handle of your briefcase—then you will be carrying your dream with you into your working week. Before you meet your difficult client or unpredictable boss or meet with someone putting you in difficult situations, write it down on paper and hold it together with your handle to be constantly "in touch" with the positive. This is an atomic step towards positivity!

Some Examples of Visualizing Skills:

- "I can code—I know JavaScript, Python, C#, C++, and Ruby!"
- "I am an expert TIG welder"
- "I'm competent to handle all challenges"
- "I can cook fantastically delicious meals"
- "I can write exquisite prose"

Visualize Clarity and Attract Positivity—Witness 3: Your Experience

It's time for the next witness, Your Experience. Visualize yourself as exuding an aura of competence and confidence. Your Experience takes the stand with complete poise and takes the oath.

The lawyer for negativity leans forward to tear into Your Experience. "What do you have to say to those who have demonstrated that the accused has no experience in their field?"

Your experience answers reasonably, "You're correct. This is a new field. But look at their experience. They have spent their careers moving into new fields, mastering them, and then moving on. They are experts at adapting and helping others to do so too. What is your point?"

The lawyer for negativity snarls, "They say that the accused is too old for the job."

"I hear that," says Your Experience calmly. "However, although they may not play computer games, they can not only use the latest technologies but also apply them expertly to solving problems."

The lawyer frowns. This witness is making good points in favor of positivity, too. It is clear that the accused has deep experience with work-related issues. He waves Your Experience off the stand.

Reflections on Your Experience at Overcoming Obstacles

Tell yourself one truthful, positive thing about your experience. Put it in your appointments' diary between every appointment. Tape it to your wrist like a pro sportsperson. Say it over and over, out aloud if you are in private! This is an atomic step towards positivity!

Some Examples of Visualization of Experience

- "I have survived worse than this!"
- "Things have always worked out so far!"
- "I know I can solve problems!"
- "I have learned many things, and I can learn another."
- "I have survived a broken heart before and come back stronger."

Visualize Clarity and Attract Positivity—Witness 4: Your Friends

This time, visualize several witnesses, all coming up together—Your Friends! They have a lot to say that is positive about you. Listen to them!

"She's not a loser, or I would not be her friend!"

"He's really clever—I ask him for advice!"

"She's a cool person—I enjoy hanging out with her!"

"He's super reliable, and he always has my back!"

Imagine the lawyer's disgust! He wants you back in the prison of negativity, but your friends can see the truth. Believe the truth about you that your friends can see, even if you can't feel it yet!

Some Questions for Reflection on Yourself as Your Friends See You

Who do you believe? Do you believe those who say negative things about you? Or do you believe the nice things your friends all recognize? Say one truthful, positive thing that your friends say about you. Keep on repeating it! This is an atomic step towards positivity!

Some Examples of Visualization of How Your Friends See You

- "I am a winner."
- "I am a good advisor."
- "I am cool."
- "I have my friends' backs."

Visualize Clarity and Attract Positivity—Witness 5: Your Potential

I hope you are getting the idea! There are so many sources that challenge your mistaken image of yourself. Here is the next witness.

Visualize yourself in something that says, "the future"! This witness is Your Potential!

Now imagine everybody staring at you as you confidently walk up into the witness box. Your Potential settles down comfortably. She knows stuff that nobody in the room has ever seen or even dreamed of.

The lawyer for the prosecution rises to question Your Potential. But the case condemning you to a lifetime of negativity and defeat is looking very weak. "Our contention," says the lawyer, "is that the accused is simply inadequate. What have they accomplished in life?"

"You stupid little man," says Your Potential. "You simply have no idea with what you are dealing with! The accused has got an immense future locked away inside, just waiting for the right time to emerge. Potentially, there are ideas and creativity, wisdom and love and compassion that would astound you. What we have here is the full value of a human being waiting to find its expression!"

Visualize the judge nodding. "Correct," she says, "I am certain that the accused is full of positive potential. Proceed."

The lawyer sits down and shuffles his papers as Your Potential returns to the witness bench.

Some Reflections on Your Potential

Tell yourself one daring, imaginative thing about your potential. Say it over and over again today. Write it on a post-it and stick it onto the edge of your computer screen to remind you throughout the day! Or slip a note into your cell phone cover that you will see every time you open it—let it intrude into every conversation you have (in the back of your mind, of course). The power is displayed on your phone, which you carry all the time. These are atomic steps toward positivity!

Some Examples of Positive Affirmations

- I feel good; I feel great!
- I am a rock!
- I am Healthy!
- My dreams have come true! (Don't say, my dream will come true!)
- I have abundant money that I need to spend in my life!

Visualize Clarity and Attract Positivity: The Point of the Courtroom Visualization

The point of this courtroom visualization drama is to take the stress off yourself. I find that if I temporarily view my life as a *game* that I am playing, I get less stressed about choosing directions and making positive decisions. Scientists have paid some attention to this phenomenon which they call "intentional dissociative behavior" (Mind, 2019). The ability to dissociate when we need a break is a sign of psychological health.

Intentional dissociation is the foundation of all techniques that people practice to calm a healthy (but stressed) mind. Two universal examples of intentional dissociation are prayer and meditation. Dramatic visualization is another example of this art of self-soothing. My theory of atomic steps aims at exactly the same thing.

It is a good thing to put a little space between you and your problem —to dissociate. Take an atomic step away from negativity and towards a positive mindset. We get so emotionally caught up in our difficulties that we can't see the wood for the trees. A dissociative visualization like the courtroom drama allows you to gain perspective.

Let me explain what the lively story of the court has brought into your life without you even realizing it.

Firstly, it has made you listen, really listen, to some sources of positivity that are perhaps hidden or submerged inside you. By bringing them to light, you are now able to think more clearly about:

- **Your ability to break negative illusions** and experience the positive truth about yourself. You have a tough Illusion Buster inside you!
- **Your possession of a unique set of skills.** Your Skilled Self has a great deal to celebrate and make good use of.
- **Your experience and memories** of how you have performed positively in the past. No matter how small the triumphs, Your Experience is an inalienably positive source of positivity.
- **Your friends** are hugely important to your advancement in positivity. They are more than just a pleasure to hang out with. Now perhaps you can appreciate what a strong positive influence they are on you!

- **Your potential.** This courtroom visualization has the potential to help you see your inner worth more clearly!

You Are the Judge—What Positive Verdict Have You Reached About Yourself?

Everything we undertake in this life is controlled by our minds, whether we realize it or not. By "mind," I mean our instincts, feelings, thoughts, and inner reflections. One of our great human powers is that we can "change our mindset." Positivity emerges from that dynamic.

The closing act of our courtroom visualization is to imagine ourselves as our own judge. A judge listens to all the evidence and decides which story is the true state of affairs. If the reason you are walking with me on this journey is that you constantly and harshly judge yourself, putting yourself down and denying yourself any hope for the future, then this is where a whole new way of seeing life can open up. The judge can change her mind!

As we continue through this week of atomic steps, you will find that the evidence for positivity becomes overwhelming! That means that by starting with visualizing a positive outer world, and moving on to visualizing a positive inner landscape, you can attract an entirely different future for yourself! That is exactly what we aim to do on our travel from Monday to Sunday

I want to stress, though, that it takes *time* to hear all your inner witnesses. Court cases typically take a long time to resolve, and you are perhaps not used to calling on these inner sources of truth about yourself. You might be so used to being negative about yourself that they are difficult to find at first! Realistically, positivity takes time to develop, which is why we need a process of small steps.

Enjoy the Journey.

Monday's atomic step is only one positive affirmation about the positive future of your outer world, or the positive truth about your inner world!

Do not be anxious that you have not been able to do everything that can be done in terms of Monday-visualization. Monday will come around again! The next step on our cyclical journey will take us into Tuesday, during which we will focus on two specific readjustments to our mindset: Gratitude and compassion.

SUMMARY

- Positive visualization has a positive effect on our minds and bodies.
- Attraction of positivity happens because like attracts like, nature abhors a vacuum, and the present is always perfect.
- We can attract positive transformation by visualizing many positive "witnesses" with us.

TUESDAY: FINDING OUR GRATITUDE AND COMPASSION?

After a long Monday, how do you feel today? Are you already exhausted, tired of all the burdens and new problems from the first day of the week? Or did you have an utterly brilliant Monday, and today seems like a bit of a let-down? Good and bad days are yin-yang in an eternal cycle, and our journey takes us through both into a positive future.

Sometimes, however, as we get into the week, we feel as if we have been dropped into a wilderness of negativity, and we doubt if we will survive. New demands and new deadlines snap at the heels of our unmet deadlines and demands. Criticism comes rolling in. Life feels desperate. It seems as if we are all alone and that nobody understands us. We fear that our mental and physical health is near collapse!

On Tuesday, the challenge is to realize you are carrying a survival pack. It is stuffed full of things of which you can be grateful for. Remember, though, that nobody expects you to tip out that bag and use everything at once. We are on an atomic level journey. The aim is to use only one survival-gratitude hack. Survive today, and tomorrow will be just that little bit better!

Insight From a Hospital Ward

Alex Kawalczyk, at the young age of 35, had a massive stroke and ended up in the hospital. The doctors warned his wife and family that he might not survive, but, contrary to expectations, he pulled through. A week after his aneurysm, he was lying awake in bed, fully conscious and deeply depressed. He was still a young man, but now his right side leg and arm were paralyzed, and his speech was slurred. He was afraid that he was facing a living hell of disability, not able to continue his work as a mechanic, and confined to a wheelchair for life. Sport, he felt, was now out of the question. He was in a deep, dark place.

I sincerely hope you do not find yourself in his circumstances. But his situation is a close parallel to the paralysis and depression many of us find ourselves in. Kawalczyk, however, found an effective way out that had knock-on positive effects in his life, and shows us how Tuesday's Journey takes us by atomic steps into gratitude and compassion.

Kawalczyk's wife showed him the way. She introduced him to the principle of gratitude. Her reasoning went like this—her husband had so many things going against him, that anything positive that remained could only be helpful. She made a deal with her stricken husband that they would both try and find as many positive things in the wreckage of his circumstances as possible. They began to look together, although neither of them expected to find much.

Their first realization was that they were grateful that Kawalczyk was alive. Secondly, they were grateful that they were in it together —"When we got married, we promised that we would do it in sickness and in health," his wife said. Thirdly, they were grateful for their health insurance, and the wonderful hospital care they could afford. They practiced a little morning gratitude ritual. Soon they realized they were grateful for doctors; nurses; physiotherapists; cleaners; administrators; technicians; and technology. The list kept growing, and Kawalczyk began to feel much more positive.

What kept the momentum of his gratitude growing was the progress he began making in physiotherapy and speech therapy. He was grateful that his slurred speech faded away. He was grateful for the little twitches of movement that began in his right leg. He was grateful for some twinges in his arm, too!

As weeks rolled into months, Kawalczyk and his wife were amazed and grateful for the amount of recovery possible. He left the hospital, and spent time in a stroke rehab center. When he was discharged from there, he could walk on both legs, with the aid of a stick. He could grasp things with his right hand, even though his grip was weak. Their gratitude accumulated with each milestone of healing. Kawalczyk's doctors told him they had never met such a positive patient, and they were sure he was powering his own healing with his attitude.

Two years later, he was playing a weekly round of golf. Sure, his swing had to be remodeled, but he was grateful to be out and about in the fresh air, on his own two feet. "I was seriously grateful for every advance," he grinned, "and for all the effort people went to look out for me. Especially my wife."

"I have learned so much through this," he added seriously. "I am especially grateful for what I have learned about my wife's true love, which included standing by me when I was in deepest trouble. She supported me day and night! I can genuinely say that I'm grateful I had that stroke."

ATOMIC GRATITUDE—A SMALL PACK OF BIG RESULTS

On Monday, we reflected on changing our point of view and visualizing a different world, both outside and inside ourselves. On Tuesday, we focus on gratitude and the compassion that gratitude releases into the world. Small inner shifts have large outward results, as the world around us is shaped by our atomic steps.

Gratitude Makes Me Feel Better About Myself

A recent survey of studies published by Harvard Health Publishing (HHP, 2021) probes the value of gratitude. Gratitude, by taking note of the positive things in your life, facilitates a connection with sources of goodness. It *retrains* your brain to realize that you are not alone in your struggles, and enables you to *feel* forces pulling you towards positivity. According to the study, "Gratitude helps people feel more positive emotions, relish good experiences, improve their health, deal with adversity, and build strong relationships" (HHP, 2021).

Dr. Robert Emmons and Dr. Michael McCullough set up a ten-week experiment to test this out, tasking one group to record "any events that affected them". The second group was required to write down every little thing that *irritated* them. The third group had to write down *only the things they were grateful for*.

Once they had done a cheerfulness test on all the participants at the end of the ten weeks of diary writing, the "Gratitude Group" were way more positive about their lives and futures. The "Grumpy Group" felt much more hopeless and way less optimistic—they also exercised *less* and visited their doctor *more* often. (HHP, 2021) Gratitude is a proven positive force for good!

See if you can relate to one of these areas to practice for Tuesday's atomic step. I don't want to give too much away at this stage, but you might find that some of the insights from Monday's exploration of visualization overlap with the insights we cover on Tuesday. I am not legalistic about order—if you want to continue working with Monday's atomic steps on Tuesday, that's fine by me!

- **Gratitude About Things I Have**

There is definitely something in there for which to be grateful about your health. Be grateful for being able to walk if you can't run. Be grateful for being able to bench press 10 kg if you can't press 250 kg.

Be grateful for having a job. If you don't have a house, be grateful for your flat. Be grateful for enough money this month to make payroll. Be grateful for the ramen in your cupboard. Be grateful for the camera on your phone. Be grateful for anything, and don't take it for granted. Say "Thank you!" from time to time when you feel grateful, even if you don't have all the things you want.

Pets are generous generators of gratitude! Your dog or cat are treasures. In a flat, you can share hospitality with a tank of fish or a turtle. Don't watch them blankly. Look at your animal companion with grateful eyes for 10 seconds, 20 seconds, 30 seconds, or a minute. Then, communicate with them with your eyes. Tell them, "I'm grateful to have you next to me to listen to me and to comfort me anytime I need you! Thank you!

We all have some nice, useful, or beautiful things. Touch one of them now and feel gratitude stirring in your heart. TREASURE and appreciate what you have NOW! Many people buy things and just put them aside, not even taking them out of the box. When you can own a thing, APPRECIATE it!

- **Gratitude About Things I Experience**

You can breathe, you can walk, you can hear, you can eat and swallow, you can jog, and you can read a book. It only takes an instant to have a little flash of gratitude for any of these things. Having a bucket list of big experiences you want in this life is a good visualization exercise, but don't let it cramp you into a negative present in which you have not yet done those extraordinary things. With a little bit of practice, one atomic step at a time, you can start getting a huge amount of pleasure in small doses from appreciating tiny things.

Look at that daisy poking its way out of a crack in the pavement! The universe is telling you that you too can thrive in the city. You can hear the birds singing, and the car horn out the back, reminding you to move the car. Your sense of smell registers wafts from cooking herbs or lavender from the garden. Be grateful!

- **Gratitude About People In My Life**

You might not have the close friends or intimate partner you desire. Give gratitude a chance, though. Consider who you *do* have in your life, and allow yourself a tiny spark of gratitude for them. A friendly bus driver or a considerate professor; a client who always tips heavily, or a waiter who always welcomes you with a smile (those two could be in a happy gratitude loop!)

If, however, you are fortunate enough to have an intimate partner and children, do not be slow in showing them your gratitude. It will build your relationship and build up both their positivity and yours.

Even if you are sick, be grateful that you have a doctor or family member taking care of you. Think about the person who cares for you, whom you might usually ignore. Gratitude helps physical healing.

Be grateful for those Messenger/WhatsApp greetings when you are down. So many people think that sending messages to greet their friends is irrelevant, and they only send work related messages. How many friends will remember you and send you a message when you are down? When they do, that's something more to be thankful for. Appreciate every little positive gesture from anyone. If you dismiss or despise these little greetings, you actually dragging yourself down. By collecting and accepting all this care from friends and family, you are accumulating positive energy. The power of this atomic journey is in the smallness of the steps!

- **Gratitude About the Future**

We all relate to the "I'm so glad tomorrow's Friday" feeling. Tuesday's atomic journey takes us one step further. Think about all the future elements of your life that are going to bring you pleasure and peace. Gratitude about the future is a kind of visualization, too. But gratitude is perhaps more focused on things you know will almost certainly happen. It's what surges in your heart when your visualizations start to become reality!

The standard spiritual advice is to live in the present and not be encumbered by the past or intimidated by the future. Gratitude, however, is a safe way to look to the future with complete positivity. Gratitude for a future that feels great and good comes to people who can dream about the kindness and positive things they will encounter. People who cannot "dream gratitude," who can only "dream success," are missing half the pleasure of a positive future. For example, imagine being grateful for a big success in your business in the future. Be grateful (although it has not yet happened) that you will be accepted at MIT next summer. Be grateful for that dream house that will be coming along in five years' time!

- **Gratitude for Our Current Circumstances**

It is vital, though, not to confine our future-oriented thankfulness to the extraordinary successes of life. We need to train our minds through small steps to enjoy the very ordinary things. Are we grateful for the skyscapes we will see tomorrow? Are we grateful for the smooth power we will be able to drive our mountain bike with on our ride tomorrow? And what about the friends we will ride with, and the companionship we will share? We will be able to pick up the next chapter in the book we are reading on Kindle. Is it time to harvest the onions in the window box? Be grateful for the feel of the soil and the crunch of the freshest onion!

Gratitude for the future does not usher in the glamorous or the magnificent (although it does so at times!). Rather, gratitude for the future ushers in a larger, richer, and wider outlook. We stop having negative tunnel vision, and begin to see our future lives as playing out on a vastly more generous scale. We are not looking for the light at the end of the tunnel (which the cynical might say is an oncoming train). No, when we are grateful, we are out in the free air, surveying the full panorama of mountains and sea and the infinite possibilities for travel. No King or Queen can do more than we can!

When Lady Gaga received her Oscar in 2019, she explained this outlook of undaunted gratitude, "It's not about winning, but what it's about is not giving up. If you have a dream, fight for it. It's not about how many times you get rejected, but about how many times you stand up and are brave, and you keep on going." (Velez, 2019) That hardy courage has to be underpinned by a positive, thankful view of the infinite possibilities of the future. And that is typical of Lady Gaga. Before she was anybody, she was always being thankful to people, as extravagantly thankful as if she were already accepting the awards that were to come later.

Are you grateful for the holiday you have booked? Are you grateful for the upcoming visit of your grandchildren? Are you grateful it's almost time for the next olympics? The future and specifically, your future, holds many pleasures. Some of them are major events, while others are more run-of-the-mill.

When you get up in an hour, you will get that fragrant cup of coffee. Mmmm! In fact, you can leapfrog the negativities of the day by mobilizing your imagination to be grateful for the next great thing coming up. Your best friend at work will welcome you like a hero. At lunchtime, you can go and sit on the terrace and enjoy the view. When you get home, you can watch that movie you saved on your Netflix account. In the traffic on the way home you can fantasize about the cocktail you're going to mix for yourself, or the walk you're going to take with your dog, and the bagel you'll buy at the bodega on the way.

With a little practice, Tuesday (and all days) can become a string of little gratitude flooding endorphins into your system during the stresses and strains of the rest of your day.

The future does not hold only trivial things to be grateful for. Your contract runs until the end of the year. Don't stress about what will happen next—instead, be grateful for the seven paychecks that are still to come. If you are working abroad, be grateful that your homeland will always welcome you back. Be grateful that your citizenship will never expire. As well as that, you have the opportunity to live abroad, and experience different cultures and cuisines. Be grateful that when you get your degree, opportunities will open up.

- **Gratitude for the Unknown Surprises That Await Me**

On that theme, be grateful for the pleasant surprises in store. Many people are afraid of the future because they fear unpleasant surprises. If you look back on your life, though, you will see that amongst the shocks there have been delightful surprises. Daydream a little about the future, then, with gratitude for the delightful shocks that await. Who knows what promotion you'll be given? Perhaps you are just about to meet that perfect intimate partner! Some big record label is about to notice your talent? Who knows!

With atomic steps into the future, gratitude can brighten a dark day and bring those surprises closer to reality.

- **Gratitude for Opportunities Opened Up by Negative Things**

This is perhaps the most important—and most difficult—aspect of gratitude. I have wrestled with this in my own personal life.

I was negotiating a deal in Thailand, back in the early days of fiber-optics. My business partner and I invested a lot of money in product design and market research. We spent many months lining up potential subcontractors, and were able to submit a very competitive bid. My partner and I spent a lot on flights to Bangkok, where we were dealing with a very large consortium, not based in Thailand but using Bangkok as their hub for the East. Everything was going extremely well, I thought.

Then everything exploded in my face! Unbeknownst to me, my partner had set up a parallel company and bid process. The Consortium knew about this, but I was kept in the dark. Out of nowhere my "partner" put in a counter-bid for the contract, using my research, data, and connections, and undercutting me by 20%. To say that it had a negative impact on me would be selling it way short! I was furious! I was incandescent with rage! Negativity poured off me and poisoned everything in a five-kilometer radius.

I felt betrayed, manipulated, and abused. There was no court to hear my complaint. I felt abandoned and bereft—and there I was with my little theory of "gratitude." It was my biggest test ever. What was there to be grateful for? I had lost my time and money. I had lost control of my research data. I had lost a business partner and a friend. And I had lost millions of dollars in potential income!

When the truth was revealed, fury almost blinded my mind. I felt utterly destroyed). I'm also a human being, and I have my weak moments. This is normal for us all!

After two or three months, though, my knowledge of the dynamics of a positive mindset brought me back. Although I was inclined to wallow in feelings of hatred and vengefulness, in the end, I could not keep it up.

I had to tackle my negative feelings little by little.

Firstly, I found that I could feel gratitude that at least this episode was over, and I could have a new beginning. That lightened my mood a fraction. There is always hope and potential in new opportunities, and I soon began to feel very grateful simply that the mess was behind me.

I still felt very negative about the partner who cheated me so badly. My recovery of a positive mindset began with a realization of gratitude. I was grateful I had found out what sort of person he was! I felt grateful that he was no longer in my life, and that I could choose better partners in future. I felt grateful that I had learned to be wiser and less trusting in business relationships. Furthermore, I had received a "degree in business ethics"—not through a university, but through what we call "the school of hard knocks."

I then realized that it was not me who had failed. I had done everything right. I had been creative and positive and full of energy. The failure was all on the part of my former partner. Yes, he had made money by abusing me. But that was a hollow victory for him. I still had my integrity intact, and for that, I was grateful.

What finally set me free from all the murky darkness and negativity surrounding that deal was when somebody pointed out a key value of that Jewish guru, Jesus. "Forgive your enemies," he said (Romans 12:13–21, NRSV). The counter-intuitive logic of that was that as I repeated forgiveness towards the man who had hurt me so badly, I felt him peeling away from my life, like a scab from a healed wound. This is really not an easy process, but when you get there, 50% of your negativity will vanish! The moment you forgive your enemy, the heaviness in your heart or mind will be lightened—you will feel as if you have had a helium boost! Hatred is so heavy. Once it has gone, it's almost as if you can fly!

I could feel my old partner's influence diminishing as time went on.. I inwardly expressed gratitude for what he had taught me, and that he had elected to show me his true nature before he did any more damage. My mind became lighter. I started being able to sleep contentedly.

He stopped being with me in my mind every moment of the day, and I stopped being his prisoner! I am deeply grateful now. It took many months, but I can guarantee you that gratitude is enormously powerful for good.

I hesitate to say this, but another thing that I am grateful for that the whole deal my former partner snatched from me went very badly. Now he is living with the fallout from that collapse. I didn't know it at the time, but my partner's cheating rescued me from a world of pain down the line. I might have gotten sucked into lawsuits and losses, or even jail time. God has plans that we will never know.

You might be in the same place, grieving a lost project, business, friendship, or profits—but you simply never know what might have been. It could be that you have deep sorrow over a broken marriage. Covid-19 might have left an indelible mark on your health. However, who knows what wonderful opportunities are yet to open up, that this loss has prepared the way for? There is always something to be grateful for, even if you have to work hard to see it.

There is always something positive in the unfortunate occurrences of life, even such negativities as divorce, sickness, or bankruptcy. In a divorce, you might be grateful for the end of a long process of shared misery, and the new freedom you have to continue with life. In sickness, as we outlined in Alex Kowalczyk's story, there are many grounds for gratitude. In bankruptcy, you get the great freedom of being able to rebuild your life better—they do say that the standard path to becoming a millionaire is having to go through bankruptcy at least once first! Having a grateful attitude trains you to find meaning in everything, as hard as that is to understand.

Life is not perfect. However, every event has its meaning. Stop and think, and be thankful for whatever makes your life complete. No one is perfect, and no one leads a perfectly happy life. With my atomic steps theory in mind, however, you will be able to accept it— whatever it may be—find the way to handle it, and face it bravely. If there *is* a solution, go ahead and transform your circumstances. If there is no available solution, accept it. The atomic journey means finding the way that makes you feel a tiny bit better. Move in that direction. You will be amazed at what unfolds.

ATOMIC COMPASSION—THE GENTLE POWER OF LOVE

Compassion Makes Me Feel Better About Myself

The flip side of gratitude is enabling others to be grateful for us! Our compassion gives them the opportunity to let all the goodness of gratitude flood their lives. Another consequence is that each act of compassion boosts our own self-esteem, and takes us one step further away from negativity. Compassion sets off a chain reaction of goodness in the world, as the person who is grateful usually delights in being generously compassionate!

Insight From a Prison Yard

Let me illustrate and explain this with a story. The poison running in almost every convict's veins is the residue of "adverse childhood experiences." Not everyone who has been beaten or mistreated ends up in prison, but most of those who do have had terrible things happen to them when they were children. 78% of all prisoners have had four traumatic, life-shaping "adverse events" in their childhood. Worse than that, 64% have had six or more gruesome and life-threatening traumas as children (McCoy, 2020). Prisons are just about the most negative places on earth.

Film producer Fritzi Horstman was herself hurt as a child, although she did not end up incarcerated. However, when she realized just how many people behind bars shared her hidden injuries, she was moved by compassion to try to do something about it.

It had to be motivated by compassion. Most of the prisoners she began to deal with were unpleasant people, hardened by repeated criminal acts. Many had done a lot of harm and evil in the world for which they had not been held accountable—they were only in prison for the things they had been caught and tried for.

Horstman is not an impractical idealist. She knows she is dealing with people who, when they get out, intend to repeat the same things that got them locked up in the first place. She has noticed, however, a key that can unlock all this miserable negativity. Compassion. Her mantra is that prisoners "are human beings, and they belong to all of us" (McCoy, 2020).

In order to bring the laser-beam of positivity into the darkest of places, Horstman founded the Compassionate Prison Project. Already there are many inmates who have been transformed by going through their programs. Apparently the cycle of gratitude and compassion is potent enough to bust even these inner chains.

I don't expect you to be a convicted felon, but even if you are, here is the way out of the negative trap you are in.

- **Compassion for Nature**

We mostly get hurt by other people, which leads us not to easily trust others. So, where can we start with steps in compassion that are small enough for an atomic journey? The answer is, in nature. We cannot change all the world's negativity. Instead, look at what we *can* do. My philosophy of Care-Think-Act asks you not to *over-think*. What small act of compassion can you show to nature today?

I pass a lady on the way to work—sometimes she plants and waters a garden on a small piece of public land. Nobody ever thought about that patch of land—it was just an ugly, weedy piece of urban negativity. If anything, it depressed anyone who noticed it. She has transformed into an astonishing explosion of greenery! Occasionally, that corner of the city now pulsates with magnificent reds and yellows, and the dusty city gusts of wind seem to turn into a countryside breeze as they pass. That might be too big a step for you or me, but I find it inspiring. Her careful cultivation of a tiny plot of ignored land shows a deep compassion for that patch of earth.

Each conscious act of compassion, however small it may be, will be an atomic step towards positivity in your life:

- Walk to the shop in the heat rather than driving your air-conditioned car.
- Pick up the trash somebody else dropped.
- Drink a soda without a straw (and save a turtle!).
- Buy and eat "deformed" carrots—much more effort to prepare, but much kinder to the earth!
- Catch a bee banging itself against a window with a glass, and set it free.
- Adopt a pet from an animal shelter, or donate to their cause.

- **Compassion for Strangers**

One of the best places to take small steps toward compassion is by taking note of strangers around us. Strangers are a good place to begin with some small steps of compassion, precisely because we have no history of them betraying our trust. We might suspect them of cheating us or of being simply too lazy to look for work. Indeed, strangers *may* abuse our generosity, but do not let that stop you from doing the positive thing *you* need to do. I find it much too easy to excuse my lack of generosity as some sort of technical kindness (I don't encourage this person's recklessness). There is a time and a place to be naively generous, even if it's only for the sake of your positive mindset.

Yes, the distressed woman who asks you for money for gas for her scooter in order to pick her child up from the hospital might just be collecting money for herself. That negative deception is *her* issue, though, and not yours. You can only come out as a winner in this scenario. Your gift has poured positivity into the world, and your heart is freer even if her heart is more bound.

Besides the people who seek to manipulate you into unreasonable generosity, however, there is a world of genuine need out there. As you gain more experience, you will find many ways to unexpectedly bless strangers who cross your path. Don't evaluate or judge people when you want to help them. Judging somebody else as "wrong" often means judging yourself, as "right"—so by over-evaluating yourself, you end up gaining arrogant pride (a negative) while losing your own sympathy or empathy!

- Be sympathetic and show a caring heart to others.
- Give a small treat to a neighbor or the people in the street
- Offer a coffee and a cupcake to someone who may not be able to afford it.
- Give a small donation to any charities you want to help. Donate when you have the ability, but don't feel guilty if finances are too tight!

- Listen attentively to an old lady's story about her childhood.

Think about how grateful you are to have this capacity to help. You will find that your kindness not only encourages others, but also lifts *your* mood.

- **Compassion for Colleagues**

People generally can not choose their colleagues to work with unless they are the Boss or the H.R. Manager. In the world of work, people often jockey for position and try to cut their workmates down. People tell lies—and let the blame for their mistakes fall on colleagues instead. But enough of that! Let's get positive.

Firstly, as you practice small steps in gratitude, you will realize more and more how many nice people are doing good things. The cleaner lady who greets you cheerfully understands the principle of random kindness! A positive reckoning of the good people and successes in your work life will free you up from your negativity. That in turn will release you to start doing small kindnesses to those who work with you. Perhaps you already do this. In that case, you already know one of the important ways to take an atomic step away from negativity.

How you show compassion to your colleagues is only limited by your creativity. Here are some suggestions:

- When you get a coffee for yourself, get one for a coworker too.
- Use post-it notes to stick compliments or positive encouragements secretly on the computers of your colleagues (occasionally).
- Take time out to attend the funeral of someone close to a colleague.
- Greet everyone respectfully, even those who curse you.
- Put in a good word for any coworker who is under pressure from management.

• **Compassion for Friends**

You have chosen your friends. Your coworkers have been assigned to you without your input! Nevertheless, it can be awkward to start taking steps of kindness towards your friends.

I encourage you to think carefully about how you relate to your friends. Are you always complaining and sharing your anger and frustration? We all do need friends who will gently listen to us when we are in difficulties. But they need you to be that sort of friend too! Perhaps you can decide that for an entire day (one atomic step) you are not going to mention anything negative and only talk about your friend's interests. Be patient and a good listener. Listening is an incredibly powerful function of friendship!

Notice your friend's likes and dislikes. Avoid talking about topics that upset them, or stirring painful memories. Compassion is knowing your friend's weaknesses, but never teasing them about their weight or singleness. Jokes that make your friend uncomfortable in any way are cruel, even if everyone laughs. Your friend will find it more and more difficult to trust you. Know the sore spots. Avoid them.

There are many little compassionate steps you can take.

- You can buy your friend the flowers she likes occasionally.
- Show up at your friend's house with some pastries he loves.
- If you are playing a game with colored counters, you can insist he gets the color counter he prefers—I know, that might sound ridiculous, but that sort of unnecessary consideration could just be the little nudge that improves his day. And it is certainly a very tiny atomic step.
- Invite your friend to join you in an activity they enjoy a lot, but that you are usually not keen on doing.
- Order something small but thoughtful from Amazon, and send it to their address. Don't wait for Thanksgiving or Christmas!

- Or you could also order nice fruit (like a small pack of cherries) or a bottle of wine from Walmart or any nearby grocery store with a delivery service.
- Most important of all, you can make yourself available when your friend needs you.

As you watch the pleasure these small acts of kindness bring to your friend, you will find something unlocking in your own heart. Nothing lifts a down mood more than watching somebody else's laughter and enjoyment. It boosts your self-esteem. It takes you one step away from focusing on your own troubles, and one atomic step closer to a positive mindset.

- **Compassion for My Family**

For many of us, this is the easiest task of all. We love our parents, siblings, and children, and they love us. It's simple to do small compassionate things for them because they are always reciprocating with compassion for us.

Sadly, a large part of the dark cloud of negative feelings in this world comes from our disappointment that those who are closest to us do not understand us, and apparently do not love us as much as we need. I am deeply sorry for your loss. However, you might be surprised at how much a renewed attempt on your part to reach out to your estranged family members brings about a positive response.

Firstly, like ourselves, our family members are only human. They too have only a limited capacity for helping themselves out of darkness. Although it does not feel like much, that acknowledgement is a significant atomic step towards positivity. This book might help them start their own journey of atomic steps. As you become gradually more positive, so will they!

What might compassion for my family look like?

- The first element is spending time. Devoting an afternoon or a weekend to a parent or a child can be the biggest gesture of compassion you could make.
- Being patient is often the key to compassion. Decide not to be rude today about how slowly your mother walks, or how slow your child is at picking up mathematical concepts.
- Allowing others the freedom to choose. Do you really know what your child dreams of becoming, or do you assume that they want to do what you want them to do? Ask your son or daughter today what they find most interesting in life.
- Treat your intimate partner to an unexpected meal or gift.

It is important that you don't tell your family members what you are doing. Just do it with a smile. If they are curious enough, they will ask you, and *then* you can explain. It might take some perseverance, though, to make the breakthrough. It all happens in tiny steps on the atomic journey.

- **Compassion for Myself**

Finally, have compassion for yourself. Some of us are merciless critics of ourselves. We cannot believe that we are good enough for anything. This has a significant influence on our positivity levels. Negative self-esteem can drive us to criticize and belittle others in order to make us feel better about ourselves. That can only become a downward spiral. Earlier, we reflected that we had several inner witnesses to convince us that we were better than that. Listen to those testimonials!

Some other readers will find that they constantly think about themselves and always put themselves first. Counter-intuitively, a conviction that they should always be first and get what they want robs them of the very positivity they crave. Compassion always needs a sort of self-forgetfulness.

I don't mean you should sacrifice your happiness to that of others, though. If you are the sort of person who always patiently listens to the complaints of your friends, and if you are *always* giving and the other side is *never* giving, then spend less time with those who drain your compassion without ever replenishing your gratitude!

We started this chapter reflecting on what might be useful to carry with you in case of emergency. If you are lost in the dark backwoods of negativity, gratitude and compassion will keep you alive!

Tuesday's atomic step is to find one new thing to be grateful for, or one new way of showing compassion.

Tuesday's reflection on gratitude and compassion puts these two humble-seeming attributes in a powerful new perspective. Next, we launch into Wednesday, where we find a vast vista of help in our quest to emerge from negativity and progress in positivity—the vision of our "tradition of insight" into the ultimate realities of the universe!

SUMMARY

- Gratitude helps us to be positive by enabling us to see positive things in our lives.
- We can be grateful for things we have, things we experience, people, the future we know, unexpected surprises awaiting us, and even for the opportunities that will emerge from unfavorable circumstances.
- Compassion helps us to be positive by enabling others to be grateful to us.

There are many opportunities to show kindness to nature, strangers, colleagues, friends, family, and oneself.

WEDNESDAY: MINDFULNESS —DRAWING FROM YOUR PRIMAL DEITY AND INSIGHT TRADITION?

You might have had a few difficulties getting going on the journey of atomic steps as we moved through "Monday" and "Tuesday." Do they work for you? Or are you wondering whether your negative mindset is too strong for you to do anything about? Due to your deep personal problems, you might have no energy or suspect the tiny steps cannot work for you.

Do not be troubled—Wednesday is a day for reconnecting with your "primal deity," whoever God is in your understanding. If you have been feeling like a very small player in a vast Cosmos, today is the day to reflect on those deep inner convictions of yours that give you a sense of meaning and purpose.

Our Insight Tradition gives us a framework for WHY we are grateful, and who or what we are grateful to, giving us an outlet for those health-giving feelings of thankfulness. It gives us a sense of embeddedness in the universe, which is essential for those of us who have a less personalized understanding of how the cosmos works. That "embeddedness," in turn, gives us the sense of security that makes compassion for others an integral and life-giving part of our atomic journey. Our Wednesday atomic steps make our Tuesday atomic steps more attainable.

INSIGHT FROM A CHILDHOOD MEMORY

Cecil Alexander wrote a poem that I learned to sing when I was a child (Alexander, 1848). It is one of the cheerfullest songs I know, and it hinges on the subject of gratitude for creation.

All things bright and beautiful

All creatures great and small

All things wise and wonderful

The Lord God made them all

What songs and poems does your Insight Tradition used to draw help you appreciate the universe in which you exist? This childhood memory reminds me to be thankful for so many things I see and experience, and this Insight Tradition opens my eyes to many positive things that my fretful adulthood tends to obscure. Alexander goes on to detail the awesomeness of great mountains, the wonder of running water, and the ever-changing majesty of sunrises and sunsets. Heat in summer, cold in winter, autumn harvests—he reminds us to look out for them with pleasure. These are things that are worth noticing and celebrating.

In addition, our Insight Tradition gives us an understanding of the future and how we relate to it. That gives us scope for the sort of hope-filled visualization that we covered in Monday's chapter.

Thirdly, our Insight Tradition helps us have courage when it seems like we are on our own with no support. The motivation of feeling that you fulfill a significant place in the cosmos gives us courage to continue putting one step in front of the other in our Journey towards a positive mindset.

The time for courage is when you are on your own—when, for some reason, your close support network is not available. It can be a lonely world if you have to struggle with negativity on your own. Get back in contact with those who can support you, even if they are only within reach via your cell phone.

Imagine the line-up before a long-distance swimming event at the Olympics. Each athlete has trained to his fullest capacity, yet many of them feel the need to turn to their Insight Tradition. Before the starter's pistol is fired, one will kneel and pray briefly. Another will chant a focusing mantra. Another will cross himself. Yet another will touch an amulet around his neck. All these men are elite athletes, but they find inner balance at the most demanding moment of their lives by bringing their Insight Tradition to mind.

If you are sad or down, Wednesday on your atomic journey is the day to let the roots of your faith guide you and give you comfort. This can have more power to bring you into a positive frame of mind than any other skill. If you have no particular religious Insight Tradition, ask for help from no-one, or the universe. You do not expect outside help, but the very act of asking puts you in a humbler position, and your suffering feels less terrible.

Although there are massive resources in our Insight Traditions, Buddhist or Sikh, Islamic or Jewish, Christian or Hindu, we tend to set them aside when we are overwhelmed by negative emotion. We get locked into the negative details of our everyday situation, and relegate faith to the margins of our consciousness. At least, that is what I tend to do. I have discovered, though, that this is a mistake. What our Insight Traditions, whatever they may be, are trying to tell us, is that there is a bigger universe out there beyond our current misery. That perspective, in itself, promotes a more positive attitude toward life.

Sometimes we need to hesitantly creep back into the circle of light, no matter how little faith we have in its permanence or validity. We are not here to discuss the deep meaning of any religion, but we understand that most religions provide a shelter that can protect us and have the power to soothe us. Keep going on the journey, and perhaps find the slimmest whisper of faith to call on your God from your inner heart. Spend time recollecting your memories of connection with your God; revisit him; seek wisdom, help, support, comfort, and more.

Whatever your Insight Tradition, they all offer something akin to mindfulness and meditation through prayers, rituals, or exercises of inner focus. Even an atheist as articulate as Sam Harris draws from his Insight Tradition when he says, "Meditation is the practice of learning to break the spell and wake up" (Anthony, 2019). Meditation has profound effects on our minds and bodies.

This is the place to get the full benefit of your Insight Tradition. Let your gods help you. Let God help you. Let Buddha, the saints, your positive mind, or the open expanse of the universe help you. Allowing yourself to accept inner help moves you to a place where you realize that at the very end of your resources, you are not yet at the end of your resources.

Insight from Napoleon's Drinking-Water Canal

Sometimes a story from history provides us with a helpful insight into mindfulness and meditation. Follow me back into the past for a little expedition into civil engineering—be patient, it will all flow together in a surprising way!

The great general Napoleon Bonaparte unknowingly offered us a helpful insight into mindfulness and meditation. Two hundred years ago in Paris, he opened his new drinking water aqueduct, the Canal Saint-Martin. (McCrum, 2016) The water, however, was soon polluted by trash. Until today, it has had to be dredged two or three times a century.

This is how it happens.

Firstly, they dam the canal and drain it to a depth of about 50 cm. Workers then trawl through the rather sludgy water with nets to catch all the fish and release them into other canals. The last time they did this—in 2001—they moved four and a half tons of bream, carp, and trout.

Then they pump out the dregs. This reveals a post-apocalyptic scene —the detritus of humanity, covered in sticky mud. There are wheelie-bins and bicycles, firearms and old tires, shopping trolleys, and broken safes discarded by robbers. It is drearily dirty and uninteresting, except for the occasional WW2 bomb (that causes a lot of excitement and the arrival of the bomb-squad).

The canal is then scraped clean by mechanical diggers and hosed clean with power-hoses. Very, very rarely do the cleaners find something actually precious, like a gold coin. Mostly, it's tons upon tons of wine bottles—this is France, after all.

Lastly, the crystal waters flow back in, the fish wiggle their way home, and for a brief interlude, the people in Paris can swim in the Canal Saint-Martin again.

That canal is my mind. That water is my consciousness, and the urban trash is the negativity that gets dumped into my life. In this Chapter 1, I would like to take you through the process of how I keep the water clear, pure, and sweet. It involves emptying and filling, but no heavy machinery.

FIRST STEPS IN MINDFULNESS— APPROACHING EMPTINESS

You and I follow different paths on this journey of emptying out the canal of the mind. There are many, many options that invite the world to enlightenment through their insights.

Ordinary people like you and me have to find our own way amongst this multiplicity of choices. For some, their choices align with their family's faith and practices down the eons. Others strike out on adventures into a new world view, under the expert guidance of a guru they trust. Still others piece together their own blend of faith and practice from many strands.

All the adherents of different ways I have spoken with agree that we share the need to put off some things and take on others in order to find *balance*.

Let me describe my adventures in mindfulness in the quest for a positive mindset. Whatever Insight Tradition you follow will offer you similar options, and I hope my observations on the process will help you calm down amid stress. At the beginning of this journey, I offered you the image of an empty glass. That can either stand for lack (nothing at all in it) or, as I prefer to see it, for potential (a receptacle to be filled). Let us continue along that line this Wednesday.

Mindfulness—Unhooking Myself From the Negative

Different Insight Traditions have simple meditative principles at their core. I have found, though, the strange inner truth that I sometimes find the negative attractive. I can see that it is causing me trouble. I understand that my negative mindset is not doing me any good. I even understand *how* to leave it behind, little by little, atomic step by atomic step. But I still do not "detach" myself. Instead, I fixate on the negative, and my mood spirals down. The negative sticks to me *much* better than the positive. Wednesday's atomic step addresses this issue too.

Insight From the Buffalo Thorn Bush

A friend of mine described an incident from his childhood in rural Tanzania that sheds light on this mysterious reluctance to let go. One of the sheep he was looking after plunged into a dense stand of buffalo thorn (Ziziphus mucronata). This dangerous thorn has numerous small, hard thorns that are needle-tipped and viciously curved. Once an animal—or even a human—blunders into the clutches of this plant, detachment is extremely difficult.

Each of the little curved thorns pierces the skin or tangles up with fur or clothing. Instantly, the unfortunate animal is securely attached to the bush by a hundred hooks. If the trapped animal struggles, as they always do, another hundred hooks latch on. If there is no one to help, the sheep gets literally dragged into the heart of the bush, where it will die from a thousand small wounds, exhaustion, and terror.

It is not unknown to come across the skeletons of animals deep in these terrible thorn bushes.

My friend says he was distraught. He ran back home across two valleys and found one of his uncles, who ran back with his nephew to see what he could do.

The terrified sheep was already thoroughly attached to the bush. Overhead, wheeling crows were wondering whether they could reach the carcass when the sheep died. Fortunately, my friend's uncle brought a steady calmness with him. The situation was dire, but he acted with a mindfulness that my friend can never forget.

Lashing a cord around one of the sheep's legs that was still protruding, his uncle got him to pull as hard as he could to stop it getting dragged further in by the wicked little thorns. If they had been strong enough to pull the sheep out, they would have simply ripped it out of its skin! I was struck by how that resonated with my idea of taking atomic steps in meditation. How often don't I try so hard that I am in danger of pulling myself out of my skin! That is not the journey we are on!

His uncle began detaching the thorns from the sheep, one at a time, cutting back the branches as he went. The rescue operation took the whole day. His uncle's arms became more and more lacerated, and his shirt sleeves became more and more tattered. Yet he went steadily on, unhooking one buffalo thorn after the other. My friend kept up the pressure, and the sheep gradually emerged. It was after sunset when they finally freed it, and the unhappy animal hobbled off to join the rest of the flock.

It's a haunting story. Like all good stories, it points beyond itself to larger truths. The journey of mindfulness is a careful, long-term process of unhooking ourselves from negative hooks.

We are not usually attached to our negativity by one great hook. We are usually attached by a hundred hooks, none of which seems like a big deal in and of itself. Where this story intersects with my theory of atomic steps is that perhaps this Wednesday you need to unhook yourself from one thorn to keep yourself from being sucked further in or to move towards being free from negativity.

In Buddhism and Hinduism this equates to the concept of "awareness," a true understanding of the true state of consciousness. Other Insight Traditions also insist that truth about oneself and the world around you is the bedrock of positive living. My friend's story shows that both he and his uncle began the unhooking of the sheep BECAUSE they had become AWARE of the problem. And that "awareness" leads us into the sort of "mindfulness" that enables us to gain freedom from the negativity that holds us back. Mindfulness is closely associated with meditation. Meditation doesn't mean you need to sit down cross-legged with your hands on your knees and a naturally curved upright spine, breathing according to the rhythm of some mantra. What my friend's uncle demonstrated was more of a mindfulness mindset. He accepted the task of freeing the sheep, and gave it the measured attention that was required. In the same way, we can do mindful art, mindful house painting, mindful iron forging, or mindful accounting.

The wisdom of relaxed mindfulness is that it enables us to do wise things because we are calm and free from panic. It takes a lifetime to master, but anyone can start on the journey and find almost immediate benefits.

Meditation Exercises—Atomic Steps in the Mindfulness of Emptying

Books on meditation often ask us to "empty the mind," but that is not easy. I prefer to suggest you start by *narrowing* your focus *to* zero. Emptying that canal came in stages! If this seems like fun, follow my three-step plan here.

- Imagine an egg. If you are more visually inclined, look up "single hen's egg" on google images. Set up your cell

phone, so there is only an egg against a black background.
Or you can go old-school and get an egg from the fridge.

- Stare at the egg for a little while, and think about what it
  brings to mind. Does your mind throw up thoughts of new
  beginnings? Or does the egg take you back to dinosaurs'
  eggs you have seen? Does it conjure up thoughts of a nice
  breakfast (sunny side up!)? Are you drawn to notice its
  smoothness, perhaps, or its color, or its weight (some
  negative people will wonder whether the egg is rotten and
  stinking inside, but we are not those people!)? Anything can
  happen in your mind. I certainly cannot dictate what you
  will discover. It could be that you see the nature of an egg
  —its shell, shape, color, and its feel in the hand. Your senses
  weigh up its "eggness," cold from the fridge or warm from
  the kitchen at room temperature, and its weight, the freight
  of life.

- That's it! You focused your vision and channeled your
  thoughts, and the single egg opened up a door into a
  wider or deeper world. Your troubles also got gently
  shelved for a small moment while you dealt with the
  strangeness of egg-meditation. We are, however, only
  dealing in atomic steps this Wednesday, so that's enough.
  Pop the egg back in the fridge or boil it up to have with
  some ramen!

Another exercise is focused on one of the "thorns" in our lives we
want to detach from. This is for when we cannot stop thinking
about our difficulties. It leads to an emptying of the mind as well,
but this time through engagement and transference. In our mostly
urban settings, it's hard to imagine getting hold of a thorn. Perhaps
on a rose from a florist? Or you could look up "rose thorn" on
Google Images, or just imagine "hooked thorn."

- Stare at the thorn for a moment. Does any interesting
  thought emerge into your consciousness?

- Can you feel something like a thorn in your daily life? Is there some irritation, sadness, or anxiety? Can you imagine unhooking yourself?
- OK, stop! That's enough for now! You can take it further next time Wednesday comes around!

As usual, this is just a starter kit. As you reflect in the right way on "Wednesday" about the things that hold you back (to detach them rather than brood on them), you will gradually create a custom-built matrix of atomic meditative steps that work for you and detach you from your own thorns of negativity.

SECOND STEPS IN MINDFULNESS—HOW REAL POSITIVITY CLEARS THE MIND

Sometimes we can only see what negatives there are in our inner beings when we have successfully detached and emptied ourselves (even a little!). Once the water has been drained or the thorns unhooked, we need to deal with the undesirable negativity that has accumulated without us realizing it! A gentle reminder: Regardless of what you are meditating on—an "egg" or "thorns"—it is okay if your mind gets lost during the process. When you are aware, you're lost, return to the "egg" or the "thorns."

"Positivity" Needs to be Worked Through More Deeply

I am completely against indulging in "unrealistic positivity." I do not deny the suffering and evil in the world. I would never tell you that your difficulties are not real. It would never occur to me to pretend that there was no such thing as Yin. It is precisely because of my sharp awareness of negativity that I understand the *need* for positivity. In the next story, we see how only realistic positivity works at clearing the mind and opening the way for good results to flow in.

Insight From Unrealistic Positivity

Let me illustrate this with a little story about two chefs working in the kitchens at, say, the Grand Mercure Ambassador Seoul Yongsan, a really fancy Korean hotel. Each of our two chefs is filling a breakfast order for an aristocratic English guest. The order is for an omelet, and the two chefs are each keen to demonstrate how skilled they are at producing English cuisine (add a touch of fresh milk, then herbs chopped and blended. Stir in some ultra-fine, unnoticeable white pepper to bring out the unique flavor. Cook until the perfect moment, and then, Voila!)

So, there they are, side by side at the long range. Butter is sizzling in their frying pans, and they each start to crack eggs into their mixing bowls.

The chef has noticed that the egg yolk color is different today... Something has gone wrong with the supply chain (or storage)! This could turn into a disaster for the special guests.

However, their reactions are different.

Unrealistically positive Chef number one says, "No, worries! It looks bad, but it is not really bad! I will not let a small negative like a "darkened" color egg yolk get me down. I deny this negativity! I will show you all! Watch me use this egg to make a superb omelet! You do not believe me, but I can work miracles." He goes on and uses that egg to make the omelet. The guest complains bitterly. Later that morning, the chef is fired. Unrealistic positivity is not only ineffective—it makes things worse.

Chef number two is realistically optimistic. Sure, he gives in to negativity for a moment when he curses at the person who gives him eggs, but he quickly snaps out of it along the helpful Care-Think-Act axis. He throws away the "doubtful" egg and cleans his work area again. Then he runs to the closest small grocery store and buys a dozen eggs. He runs back, cracks the fresh eggs, makes the omelet, and serves it up a little late but perfectly cooked. The guest raves about the omelet. The face of the manager is fixed. Later that morning, chef number two gets promoted to Sous-chef!

We need positive thinking *because* negative situations arise. Our positive *attitude* releases positive *energy* into our lives. And that positive energy sweeps out the problems and negativities in the most effective way possible. This is the equivalent of the power-hoses in the cleaning of the canal! When we discover that the batch of eggs is off, we get rid of them and actively replace them, which will lead us into our third aspect of mindfulness, choosing to fill our minds with the positive.

Meditation Exercise—Atomic Steps in the Mindfulness of Attitude

For this exercise, we need a candle. Many Insight Traditions use candles to help their adherents achieve balance and positivity through various techniques. The technique I recommend is simple observation and reflection.

- Make yourself comfortable and light a candle, placing it in the middle of a clean sheet of paper. It could be a real candle, or if you are on a train or airplane, it could be imaginary, or a GIF file on your cell phone.
- Observe or imagine the flickering flame and the slight wisp of smoke.
- Write your most intense problem on a small slip of paper.
- Focus on the candle flame and imagine a positive outcome for the problem.
- Burn the slip in the candle flame (actually, or in your imagination!)
- As the paper flares, look quickly down at the blank sheet of paper and write down a positive outcome that comes to mind.

That's it! It's more elaborate, but it carries a lot of promise for positivity. Your worst problem is symbolically gone, and your best outcome is written down for further reflection and action!

That exercise in mindful meditation leads into the third step of mindfulness—refilling the emptied and cleansed canal of consciousness.

THIRD STEPS IN MINDFULNESS—BRINGING BACK THE CLEAR WATER

Now we come to the filling of the canal with clear drinking water, and the return of fish and people to a sparkling new reality. We have taken a journey towards emptying and unhooking. As we proceed on our atomic journey, meditation allows positivity to flow into our lives. It is very important that we limit the number of negative things that will want to flow back into our minds. I find that if I am very intentional about positive influences at this point, I emerge from my "Wednesday" with a better mindset than I entered it with.

According to Angela Ruth, drawing on the work of Dr. Loretta Breuning, the human brain can generate more than 50,000 thoughts per day! This is a dangerous overload that can lead us to burnout! Ruth suggests that there are a number of important ways to ensure that amongst everything we think there is a positive flow of energy into ourselves, and she recommends a sort of mindfulness that is very similar in objectives to my seven-day Journey. Her "techno-mindfulness" steps are:

- Ask yourself, "What am I thinking?"
- Choose two or three of your most positive thoughts and think about them some more!
- Contact someone for pleasure or compassion (not for business!)
- Help someone else. Don't think about it. Just do it.
- Spend as much time as you can with people who build you up.
- Rest, reflect, and eat healthily.
- Make time to do something you love (Ruth, 2022).

Ruth quotes Dr. Breuning's pertinent comment—"Our brain evolved to promote survival. It saves the happy chemicals (dopamine, serotonin, and oxytocin) for opportunities to meet a survival need and only releases them in short spurts, which are quickly metabolized. This motivates us to keep taking steps that stimulate our happy chemicals." (Ruth, 2022) The journey we are following through the week offers us an unlimited supply of dopamine, serotonin, and oxytocin-generating steps!

Wednesday's atomic step is to practice a single element of mindfulness.

On Wednesday, we investigated the positive power of mindfulness and meditation, as they are embedded in our own personal Insight Tradition. Let's carry the learnings of the first three days of the week into Thursday, where I would like to introduce you to the vital dynamic of disconnection—actively switching off the negative in order to promote a positive mindset.

SUMMARY

- Wednesday's atomic step challenge is to explore the mindfulness and meditation methods of your Insight Tradition.
- Meditation involves emptying out the negative and pouring in the positive.
- By avoiding unrealistic positivity, we can unhook ourselves consciously, one by one, from the things that hold us back.
- We can end our Wednesday more positively if we actively "soak" in positive influences, flooding our lives with positivity.

THURSDAY: DISCONNECTION AND THE CLOAK OF INVISIBILITY

Has the week been wonderful so far, with things happening beyond your expectations? Or has it been a bit of a bust, and you have found it hard work to move steadily forward, taking atomic steps into positivity?

One great trigger of negativity for me is traffic. It seems as if the whole world becomes an obstacle to my car—I am connected to a million cars, and I long for an open road. Can you relate? Perhaps you feel those feelings of over-connection when you have to queue at a government office. Are you driven to irritation by a specific person at work who will not stop teasing you? Is there a worksite bully who is always trying to get you into trouble with the supervisor? Is there a creepy teacher who you feel very uncomfortable with?

Over-connection leads to stress and exhaustion. These are not positive things, and like the bad egg in the omelet, we cannot make them positive as such. I have had to learn how to disconnect from this negativity, and in doing so, I have developed atomic step approaches for when I do not want to be where I am right now. One is through *avoidance*. I travel early or late, at times when traffic is light. Or I avoid the traffic by stopping, parking, and sitting and watching the waves of the ocean, the leaves stirring in the wind, or sipping coffee in a café. The second is by *imaginative disconnection*— entering an inner alternative reality while remaining perfectly in control of the stream of traffic. Both of these are forms of useful dissociative behaviors (Mind, 2019). Both are good for my inner positivity.

DISCONNECTION: AM I ALLOWED TO NOT BE AVAILABLE?

Let's start with a joke. There once was a man who turned off all his electronic devices for 24 hours.

That's the joke (in case you missed it!)

Nobody in their right mind would fast from electronic devices! The audience roars with laughter, and the stand-up comedian mentally ticks that off as one to keep using. The idea is ludicrous in our post-modern context! The cell phone, iPad, and computer, are the defining cultural objects of our era. Not having a "device" at hand is as absurd as wandering onto the stage without your trousers!

Many people are happy to be online all the time, chatting, shopping, or watching funny TikTok or YouTube videos. If that's your jam, I am not intruding on you. My concern is for those of you for whom the open electronic gate into your life has become a source of stress and negativity.

Am I allowed to take off my pants in public? *Am* I allowed to turn off my devices?

Business, entertainment, personal organization, communications, and other relationship maintenance functions are all mediated by the little gadget in our purse or pocket. It would be shockingly absurd to think of disconnecting!

Don't disconnect *me* at this point! There is more to the story.

Our whole lives are lived through the avatar of our cell phones, and negative forces consistently attempt to hijack them! Think about it.

Commercial AI is constantly manipulating our minds with its sneaky cookies and algorithms. One negative tweet from you, and the algorithm dumps an avalanche of related negativity into your feed in order to make money out of your misery! Disconnect yourself from technology whenever you can.

Your attention is bombarded by negative memes, dismissive tweets, and mocking or furious messages. Many advertisements offer you dubious products or services that will never make your life more positive—and will make your bank account depressingly negative. Some people feel empowered to be vicious and unkind with their allocated characters, and they can do twice as much damage in 280 words as they used to in 140! Negative images flood our senses—what is it with Dickpics anyway? And does my visualizing mind *have* to fight visions of mangled bodies and human cruelty? Add to that the people who insist I have to stay in contact with them—that repulsive uncle or that overly demanding boss or my mean ex—and the attraction of switching off becomes greater.

There are some very negative forces out there that insist on you staying connected to them, so they can pour out their venom by complaining, demanding, and guilt-tripping you. One of the things they say is that it is not responsible or adult to turn off your devices. Being out of the cyber-loop is failing to fulfill your duty to humanity, your duty to always be available "in case of emergencies." Often, what they really mean is that they want you at their beck and call. That boss who wants to be able to phone you out of office hours—why? Why does that creepy neighbor have to be able to contact me in case of an emergency? Why does that friend who constantly pours out bitterness and complaints have a right to monopolize me for an hour on Saturday when I just want to be chilling with a new book or movie?

Not only does your rest get interrupted, but also your relationships with others, and your own self-care. The negativity of being always on call is there even if there are no phone calls on the weekend. Your mind has a nagging anxiety that a negative stressor *might* phone, and that is one extra little hook into negativity you don't need.

Atomic Steps in Disconnection through Avoidance

If you feel too guilty to switch off completely, here are some questions that might guide you.

- Are the people who want you to be constantly available, those who bring positivity into your life?
- Are they people who lighten your mood or darken it?
- Are they people who demand more than you can give?
- Do they have power over you, like bosses, supervisors, or show directors?
- Then you must ask yourself whether they *should* have that control over you!

Once you have clarified that you are not automatically guilty, and that you are indeed allowed to "switch off," here are some hacks for disconnecting yourself from negative triggers. One of these might make a big positive difference on this Thursday of our journey

- Switch off. Switch off all media for planned and limited periods. Take respite breaks. Not forever, but for however long you need to recover from being harried by other people's priorities.
- Spend time in a museum, soaking up beauties of shape and form. Or dawdle past an art shop and absorb beauty for free. Spend some time pondering what artwork you might value as a permanent fixture in your home—this is a lovely visualization exercise.
- Chill out with that wine and movie!
- Can you outfox your whiny, negative, energy-sapping tormentors? Lock your phone in your locker at the gym, perhaps, or give it to your taxi-driver dad to ride around with all shift. Then you could genuinely say "My phone

was at the gym," or "My phone was in a taxi all night, but I got it back in the morning." The great general Sun Tzu would be proud of you. You have taken a very positive atomic step. If you have to fight to not get dragged down into negativity, you have put into action his observation that "all war is based on deception" (Sun Tzu, 2013).

Having said all that, though, there might be some people for whom you genuinely *must* be available 24/7. Do you have a parent in a care facility, and you want to be on hand if something happens? Do you have a child traveling overseas, and being on call makes you feel less anxious? Do you have a bid on a business deal that might need some last-ditch defense against your competitors? Are you in the medical or first responder worlds, where instant response is vital? You have convinced me. Do *not* turn off your phone. Can you not mute anything other than those particular numbers, though? That would be an atomic step *towards* disconnection. It might result in big benefits for your inner life, too.

DISCONNECTION THROUGH IMAGINATION: THE CLOAK OF INVISIBILITY

Sometimes push comes to shove, and you cannot avoid your negative stressor. You and your difficult ex both need to attend your child's award ceremony, for example. My strategy is to make the encounter as brief and distant as possible. Or, like Harry Potter wearing an invisibility cloak, go to the event and say a quick hello to your kid with a kiss. Then, shimmy out before anyone realizes that you've disappeared.

It is never possible to totally avoid all the people who funnel negativity into your life, especially if they are relatives—and in that case, you do really need the "invisibility cloak." You will not always be able to withdraw yourself from the scene of conflict or the locus of negativity. Imagine you have a colleague you dislike, who always gives you a hard time, or an enemy who has hurt you. They work in the same open-plan office as you, and you are assigned to work on several projects together. Tomorrow, once again, you will have to face them and interact with them. Their faces are always in your mind, and you feel annoyed and uncomfortable. Harry Potter inherited a cloak of invisibility from his father. As you gloomily eat breakfast, you wish with all your heart that you had one, too.

You do!

It's invisible before you put it on, and you can use it in two ways. You can throw it over yourself and make yourself disconnected. Or you can throw it over your opponents, and make them magically disappear. As they say, "out of sight, out of mind." for the sake of your inner health and wellbeing, you have to break the hostile eye-contact between you. This magic cape is a new application of something we have reflected on before—visualization! In this case, perhaps "de-visualization." Here is how to deploy this magical cloaking device in two steps.

"Disappearing" In Plain Sight—

Step 1: Imagine yourself relaxed and in good spirits with this person who holds a grudge against you. The vibes are positive, and both of you are smiling. It is a strange thing to try, but try it anyway. It is extremely hard, but give it a go anyway—the science of cheerfulness points out that even a fake smile cheers you up! (Verny, 2022) It is a specific form of visualization that envisions future happiness in order to help it arrive. Rescript your usual interactions completely. Pleasantness is your specific, visualized intention. Magic will happen! Only think about the *pleasant*.

Step 2: Place yourself in the center of a circle drawn in your imagination. Draw it in your journal, if that helps. In your mind, pull the negative person into the circle with you. This is the circle of your power, however, which nobody can challenge. Draw a smaller circle around your opponent within the larger circle. Then imagine yourself grabbing hold of that little circle and dragging your opponent far away from you, where you can't hear them or even see them. Do this while you are on the way to work, and you'll arrive at a transformed workspace. Nothing has changed outwardly. You are both still in the same office. The negative person is still as negative as ever. You, however, are serene because you have redrawn reality to suit yourself!

Even the smallest step towards this positive visualization will be rewarded by an improved mood. The hostility of this colleague will cease to have any effect on you. Yes, he might still be as mean as ever, but you have placed him in a place where he can no longer grind you down into negativity. Another benefit is that you can keep on relating over work issues, which will benefit you, him, and anyone else involved. So this little technique prevents them from screaming and berating you when they are not even in earshot. You have gotten them out of your mind.

This technique can also help you sleep better if you have been traumatized or thrown into a spell of negativity by some event, even if it's a disaster you caught on TV or something bad that happened to your child or someone else you love. Lasso this event or a person with your mind, or drag the event or someone out to a distant place. Then, you can even put a "Cloak of Invisibility" on this event or person to have it disappear. That will give you the freedom to sleep, and that in turn will work its healing magic on you.

On Thursdays, this can become your signature maneuver—encircling and removing the stressors, personal and impersonal, that lower your mood. Miracles happen, even if we have to work for them slowly. Your miracle can start happening tomorrow.

If negativity is bubbling up destructively in your family, with opposing agendas for parents and children or brothers and sisters in conflict with each other, why not sit down together and work through the "atomic steps" theory, helping each other to choose tiny steps to take towards positivity and wholeness. It could transform your home environment. Are things not going so well between you and the love of your life? Be open with each other and discuss things. In the long run, two negativities together will hurt deeper. Invite your intimate partner to join your relationship-healing seven-day journey.

Try it with your friendship circle too, if things have been getting too competitive or domineering, and things aren't going so well anymore. Work through the week of atomic steps and see if it refreshes the positivity among you.

POSITIVE DISCONNECTION STRATEGIES

Insight From an Itinerant Rabbi

Jesus was very aware of the need to disconnect—he knew the importance of managing the connections he made with people and when to move on to new relationships and tasks. In Mark's Gospel, there's an account of one morning when Jesus was alone, recharging himself with prayer before sunrise. The previous day had been hectic. His disciples came and disturbed him, calling him down to the village to carry on with his teaching and healing there.

Jesus refused!

His disciples were confused. Was their rabbi refusing to help people who needed him? Jesus, however, calmly led the disciples on to the next village, teaching the disciples an important lesson in husbanding their resources of time and energy, and spreading the horizons of their love (Mark 1:34–39).

There are various techniques and strategies for making yourself unavailable. We have discussed an important aspect of this—turning off our phones. But there are other instances where you might want to withdraw from people or activities. Here are some of the situations where this technique has worked well for me.

Don't Let Invisible Social Media Strings Control You

I am not saying do not use contemporary technologies. What I am saying is that if you are struggling with your battle against negativity, one tiny positive atomic step might be the slight pressure of your thumb on the off switch.

There. You are now disconnected.

Take a break—even a ten-minute break—and use it to reflect on what things, services, and people on your cell phone are "bringing you joy," as Marie Kondo says (Kondo, 2022). If there are people, groups, or sites to delete, imagine the peace and positivity that a little decluttering will bring.

OK, now you can switch back on!

I bet that nobody noticed your ten-minute absence. As you reflect on that, try and expand your boundaries to carve out dedicated, positive "me" time. If you do get challenged for missing a call, you can apologize briefly and get on with your life. The truth is that the relief of being free from the demands of your phone will outweigh any possible friction it might cause.

Cell phones are not the only element of our lives that we might need to disconnect from. I say "need" on purpose here because if you don't establish some distance from certain influences, you are not going to be able to extricate yourself from a negative downward spiral. If you know that you are a people-pleaser, especially, you have to do some of this "cutting off" work for your own wellbeing.

Thursday is the day we reflect on this cutting-off process and its potential to provide atomic steps towards positivity.

Switch Off the News

Avoid the news, for one. Psychologically, people tend to be more interested in news about disasters, and unhappy, unjust, unfair, and tragic events. As we have discussed, five out of six of our emotions prime us to pay attention to what might harm us—and the news only offers us disaster to look at. This sells news because arousing topics and controversy increases the viewer rate and boosts the channel's income. The more we expose ourselves to such news, the more negative we become.

I myself love watching news on YouTube, but I think I'm addicted to his channel. Yes, I love the insights—but sometimes I ask myself to disconnect. I find the negative orientation of the news affects my mood unnoticeably. Media outlets are offering us negative atomic steps! Let's fight back with some positive ones for our journey.

Atomic Steps in Disconnecting from Electronic Media

- Off button. Consider it!
- Only watch for culture, sports, and the weather.
- Switch channels to something super-positive. I like watching African wildlife on Wild Earth or cooking channels.
- Rely on Netflix to bring you comic relief and romance.

Disconnect by Walking Out and Walking Away

A colleague starts telling a racist joke that he mistakenly thinks everyone will find funny. This makes you sad and, to be frank, a little disgusted. So, what can you do? You can stay in the circle of friends, listen through the joke, and smile awkwardly, pretending to find the joke amusing for the sake of maintaining social cohesion. In some situations, especially where the colleague is senior to you, this might be a wise thing to do.

It costs you, though. You lose a little self-respect, in that you have pretended to approve of something you find unacceptable. That's a negative hook in your soul. Another negativity hook is that you now despise this colleague a little, and that in itself is an unwelcome emotion that you do not want to keep and have to disguise, which does not lead to positivity. There is also grief in that mix—sorrow for the racial group that is earning your colleague's scorn through his joke. "It's only a joke," some people argue. You, however, who understand the importance of the words we use to construct our worlds, know that jokes often reveal the truth of the inner world of the joke-teller. They reveal what he thinks, believes, and values (or devalues). Whatever the case, you are now feeling jaded and in a worse mood than when you entered.

Another reaction, depending on your personality, is to stand and speak up. Some people can do this with rough good humor. "Shut up with all your racist crap!" you say, but somehow you have the personality that makes it not only inoffensive but sets the whole pub laughing instead. "Tell a better joke, or next time I'll turn up with some of my friends (from the race group being derided)." Everyone roars with laughter, and also a bit of anxiety because everyone knows the sort of people this straight talker hangs out with. It also costs you, however. Despite your big personality, you have had to use all your social power to shut down something you hate. It spoils your evening and leaves you with deeply hidden anger, which acts like acid on your mood and positive outlook. Disappointment corrodes.

Don't do this if you do not have that big a personality; people will attack you as "someone who can't take a joke." Things might even end in a barroom brawl. That would leave you in a negative mood, nursing anger *and* bruises. If you are already weak at managing your negative mindset, you are in danger. The more you expose yourself to them, the more you are harmed without noticing!

Atomic Steps in Disconnection: Walking Out and Walking Away

Consider the following hacks and tactics. One of these might be this Thursday's atomic step for you.

- Head off to the toilet.

- Or quietly pay your tab and go out to call an Uber to your hotel. You don't need to explain yourself—people are always coming and going in bars.
- You could also pretend to have received a text that requires your urgent attention. The positive result is that you have taken an active step to preserve your own possibility.
- Say to yourself as you leave, "I don't have to listen to somebody else's negativity."

There are many situations like this where I take evasive action. If a friend, colleague, or relative calls me, and I know they will spend the next half hour pouring out hate and discontent about the world in general, expecting sympathetic agreement from me, I have a rock-solid strategy in place to preserve my positive mindset. I turn my phone into flight mode, and the call mysteriously disappears without the caller knowing that I have shut it down.

Disconnection by Avoidance

A visiting dignitary whom you suspect of being involved in corruption drops by to "chat" with people at the office. You hate spending time with this individual, with his constant hints about how he can make your planning application go more smoothly if you can only reach "some sort of (unspecified) agreement" with him. You simply tell your secretary to tell him you were called away on urgent business. Meanwhile, you slip out through the back door and end up feeding the pigeons on the pier. Well, it was urgent—pigeons need to eat, too. Now you feel positive and happy, with the sun on your face, the wind in your hair, and grateful birds massed around your feet.

Of course, not many of us have the authority to stiff a visitor like that. If, however, the person in question has a regular appointment, it is a matter of simple logistics to schedule other work elsewhere for yourself.

Atomic Steps in Disconnection by Avoidance

- Find a coffee shop nearby, and calm your brain with the sensory balm of coffee. I often refer to aroma and smell. It's a wonderful remedy. More of that on Sunday! Now, let's continue this Thursday journey.
- Save up all your out-of-office work assignments for those specific times when you expect a stressful person to show up, and simply be absent.
- Let your colleagues with more emotional bandwidth interact with negative people. It is important to maintain a positive mindset.
- Find a quiet place outside (with the smokers, perhaps—they are experts at finding quiet hidden places outside!) and read through "Thursday" on your Kindle.
- Listen to the audiobook version of this book while packing shelves or doing some other deep background activity.

Disconnect by Displacing Stress Triggers with Peace Triggers

One of the best approaches to disconnection is to replace the negative with a positive. In the case of the tense situation at the bar it is much better, if you can, to hang out with people who like you for yourself, and are not trying to project their own dominance onto society. Good friends will be sensitive to your sensitivities and will not joke about things you find offensive. Make sure you actively embrace any offers of friendship from people who are on the same wavelength as you—this is the sort of relationship where you can both give and receive positivity!

Atomic Steps in Disconnection by Displacement

- Leave your negative friends and spend your lunch break or time after work with your positive friends.

- Accept any offer of friendship from nice people. Do not hold yourself aloof!
- Even if you're feeling down, accept invitations from friends who make you feel better. Don't say no! Get positive vibes from positive people.

Pruning People from Your Past

I once had a lesson from a peach farmer on how to graft high quality fruit-bearing branches into hardy (but undelicious) stock trees. His right forearm was as massive as my thigh from a lifetime spent endlessly operating secateurs. Do you need to develop *your* forearm? Does your positive mindset depend on some focused pruning of your contact list?

Who are these negative triggers? You know who *yours* are.

- The young men you used to hang out with, and who encouraged you to do crime with them.
- That ex who is consistently mean and unresponsive about childcare issues.
- Those old army buddies—whenever you meet with them, your PTSD flares up, and you have a week of combat nightmares. The same goes for reunions of many sorts.
- In another vein, perhaps you feel heart sore whenever you glimpse the former love-of-your-life who rejected you and chose someone else. Long buried feelings of envy and anger spoil your entire day.
- People hurt each other, and sometimes they carry those scars for a long time before they can forgive our way out of captivity.

Atomic Steps in Pruning

This Thursday, you can work out some atomic steps to become part of your recovery ritual for whenever you have to re-disconnect with people from your past. Firstly, there are three general principles I find helpful for Thursday disconnections:

- Put some distance between you and the stressor. Don't hang out with your ex, no matter how committed you are to "being friends."
- If somebody brings extreme stress into your life, or even danger, getting a court order could be an appropriate atomic step to take this Thursday.
- Practice some of the conscious forgiveness skills we've reflected on.
- Trim your digital contact lists. You do not have to be in touch with these stressors, or even those people you only contact to find out how your ex is faring. Delete, delete, delete!

Then there are several "replacement" suggestions—putting yourself someplace where people cannot reach you to break you down. I find that quietness calms me down and cheers me up. You might have the opposite personality and need to be cheered up before you can calm down!

- Go for a run or gym session.
- Make and eat some comfort food.
- Bury yourself in a book, a hobby, or a TV series.
- Have a leisurely visit to a museum.
- Visit a bookstore. It does not have to be a new-book store. Pre-owned books have their own healing charm.
- Go for a silent walk in nature.
- Spend some time cuddling with your pet.
- Go to a music concert and rave yourself better.

If none of these suggestions floats your boat, that's OK. Thursdays are the day for planning disconnection strategies that work for *you*. The direction of your atomic journey is always *your* choice because you are your unique and wonderful self.

Thursday is when you can focus on plans and tactics for removing yourself from people who stress you out, avoiding them, or coping with them. An atomic step for today could be to think about somebody you don't want to spend time with this week, and work out how you can avoid them.

Thursday's atomic step is to practice a single step of disconnection.

We have investigated and started to apply simple steps towards disconnection from the negative on "Thursday." "Friday" is next. We are going to take a frank look at "ugly" negatives and work out how to acknowledge them and then put their influence behind us. We shall search for the hidden treasures in this dark mother lode.

SUMMARY

- Switching off (disconnecting from) all your electronic devices and TV for a short time can be a stimulus for positivity.
- Get back to nature
- Develop withdrawal strategies for managing people-stressors
- For those, you can't avoid, use "invisibility-cloaking" strategies to escape notice.
- Use the lasso and remove tactics for coping with in-your-face negativity.

FRIDAY: HOW TO SAY HELLO TO THE NEGATIVE

You're looking good, although perhaps you feel a little tired. Does the prospect of the weekend fill you with deep relief and great anticipation? I hope so. Thank God, it's Friday! After the small steps of learning to maintain your positive equilibrium on Thursday by physically and psychologically disconnecting yourself from stressful people and actively cutting off negative influencers, there is one more step to freedom that we will focus on "Friday"—saying hello to the negative.

If you are like me, you have unintentionally accumulated a lot of negativity in the past week. On Fridays, we typically evaluate our working week. Machele Galloway, a life-coach and dog-lover, suggests that there are only two questions you need to ask—what went well, and what did not go well (Galloway, 2020). In my week of atomic steps, I don't want to specifically analyze the working week, but I do recommend that we take stock of both the positive and negative influences that have come to bear on our minds. Friday is the day for dealing with the negative in preparation for a crazy-positive weekend!

Let's say hello to the negative—and goodbye!

GREETING THE NEGATIVES IN MY LIFE

Most of us can relate to Bianca's story. Some weeks are just like that! Here's what happened.

Insight From a Working Mom's Week

It was tough being a single mother, and her ex-husband was stalling on payments for things their children needed. That Monday, they had met each other with lawyers to settle their latest dispute. She had burst into angry tears. He had sat there, icy and unmoved. Bianca sighed. How could one person disappoint another so badly? She almost threw a heavy file at him. He smirked.

On Tuesday, nobody on the team picked up on the mistake in the financial calculations, although Bianca had felt that something was not quite right. It was the first thing the boss noticed. The entire report had to be reworked. There was an unpleasant hour of shouting and blaming. Then the team had to crowd together in a boardroom and redo a week's work. It was almost midnight before she got home.

On Wednesday, her former husband's parents, grandparents to her two children, had visited. They still blamed Bianca for the split, despite their son's multiple adulteries. Her mother-in-law found an expired tin of soup at the back of the grocery cupboard and spent half an hour berating Bianca for "poisoning her grandchildren." When they left, Bianca had to call her closest friend to unload.

Thursday, her son had fallen and broken his leg at school. In between soothing her frightened child in the ER and calling in help from a friend to pick up her daughter from school, her line manager called furious with her for missing a meeting!

Today had not been a marvelous Friday either. She called to tell her classmates she would not be attending their reunion. Her closest school friend told her she was selfish to prioritize family over friends. Bianca had rung off, irritated. She felt completely exhausted.

Bianca is, very naturally, feeling quite down this Friday. As she recalls the negative things that happened and the negative emotions she felt, she perhaps wonders whether this will be another depressing weekend. It doesn't need to be if she can develop immunity to negativity.

Developing Immunity From Negativity

What Bianca needs—along with all of us—is some way of neutralizing the negative experiences she is carrying in her heart. Nature has a mechanism for dealing with pathogens that infect the body. White blood cells, which are constantly being generated in our bone marrow, actively hunt down any virus or bacteria that enters our system. After a brief battle (during which we might experience some symptoms like headaches, a temperature, or body pains), the defense system of our body overcomes the invader, and we are well again. We are, in fact, more than well—as part of the healing process, our body takes note of the shape of the dead cells, and establishes immunity from further attacks. No more illness from the same germ! If it crosses our path, it can have no further effect on our bodies.

In the same way, atomic steps towards positivity can interact with negative influences and not only make us feel more cheerful but also prevent us from feeling so broken down by negativity in the future!

First, however, our positive self must first meet the negative "virus" and call it by its name. It is only if a doctor knows what virus she is dealing with that she can prescribe the appropriate vaccine. In the same way, we need to courageously "meet and greet" the negative things that have troubled our lives.

How to Say Hello to My Week's Negatives

Bianca, in our story, has a certain portfolio of negatives. Of course, you might have entirely different negativities, but on our atomic journey, I suggest you try this mini-positive mindset process.

After setting her kids to sleep, Bianca sat relaxing on the couch, hugging one of her daughter's teddy bears in her lap. She took a deep breath in her chest. The music of Satie's Gymnopaedia flowed around her and into her. She was rewinding the week's events in her mind. Friday was her day to say "Hello" to her week's negativities, challenges, and unhappiness. She could still feel the pain and tears, but now she was calmly changing her relationship with those negatives.

"Hello, Ex," she said in her mind. Her big Monday negative shuffled in. "You were the one I loved and trusted, but you betrayed me and hurt me deeply. I hated you! Dame it!" said Bianca in her mind. She exhaled a vital breath and continued, "However, I forgive you! Although you yelled at me again this week. It's okay. I'm fine, and you did not break my spirit. I put all my negative thoughts about you aside. My mind is more robust than you thought. I can do hard things for the sake of my children."

Satie's elusive melodies teased out the tangle of her mind. "Hello Boss, I respected you and always gave my best to you. You brought anger, resentment, and shock to the office. You caused difficulties, expense, and exhaustion. But you didn't win; you couldn't break us. So, our team spirits have become more robust than ever! Your resentment and anger will no longer affect my team and me."

Bianca sips her camomile tea. She continued to rewind her horrible Wednesday's memory with her former husband's parents: "Hello, Papa Joe, and Mama Anne. Every visit from both of you has brought me frantic disorientation and anxiety. You blamed me for everything, including how badly I treated my husband and your grandchildren. I feel humiliated like no one else. But, despite this, with my sympathy and mercy, I forgive you. I didn't defend myself because I wanted to protect you and didn't want to stimulate your hypertension. Suppose you felt better after making complaints about me. Please do. You can't damage my mind. I have the best support from my parents and my children!"

After injecting positive thinking into her unpleasant incidents, Bianca felt much better and more relaxed. Now, her Wednesday's Anguish appeared in her mind: "Hello, worry! You tried to defeat me on Wednesday, causing trouble for my son, my daughter, and my work. But you didn't! I'm so proud of myself, son. The doctor told me my son was one of the bravest kids he had ever met. My son held my hand tightly and didn't yell a word during the painful inspection. I felt his quiet but powerful support. I learned a great lesson from my son!

Now, Bianca walked to her bathroom and washed her face. In front of the mirror, she rewinds her negative mindset that just happened a few hours ago. "Hello, frustration. You tried to blame me with no sympathy and bombarded my dignity and pride. You are just using words, and you can't hurt me physically. I know I'm doing the right thing for my family. You can't destroy me because my mindfulness mindset is my most vigorous shelter."

Bianca smiled to herself in the mirror as Satie's Gymnopedia caressed her spirit with "We'll float off up to the stars" (Satie, 2019).

Now her negative influences had lost all their power. She has survived the worst negatives the week could throw, emerging cheerful and decomposed.

As a footnote to Bianca's story, let me assure you that I find it to make perfect sense. I never deny adverse events or the negative reaction I have to them. For me, "Friday" is a day for taking a step towards acknowledging, befriending, and confronting negativity bravely. We are complex beings, and in the same way that a virus can be turned into an antiviral mechanism, so our negative experiences can be turned into anti-negativity elements in our lives!

As we face our negativity, each courageous meeting will greatly rebuild our confidence. The more our small minds talk about negatives, the braver and more joyful we become. Hello Negative! I've got my eye on you!

GENERAL HELP WITH YOUR MEET-AND-GREET WITH NEGATIVES

Bianca was brave enough to really look at the negatives in her life. As they came out of the shadows, they looked less terrible. She was able to befriend them all, and they ended up helping her become more positive about life. She had put many sensible psychological recommendations into practice.

I am indebted to Dr. Leslie Ralf for assistance here from her clinician's notes. She has helped countless people stuck in the doldrums find positive forward momentum in life (Ralph, 2022).

- Tackle negatives one at a time. Bianca greeted her Negatives one by one at a time. Like that jackal we referred to earlier, the meal has to be eaten one bite at a time. The journey requires only one step at a time.
- Make sure the negative really *is* a negative. The pain of her son breaking his leg helped him develop a sense of responsibility, so it became the foundation of a surprisingly wonderful positivity. Don't be hasty in condemning yourself, either!
- Keep your cool and hold yourself back. Bianca's tears only played into the hands of her resentful former husband. On the positive side, she did not throw the file at him!
- Remember that you deserve treats, attention, and praise as well—the cure for a disastrous week is not to punish yourself. You are not guilty here. Bianca earned her leisurely, splendidly quiet night with her favorite piano music. What do you deserve?
- Pay attention to your gut. Your intuitions might be warning you of something that you do not consciously know yet. Bianca had an instinct that the report was flawed!
- Guard your memory. One negative tends to recall all the other similar negatives you have had. For example, Bianca struggled in her meeting with her ex because she could

recall all his previous cruelties. This applies to all your old anger, fears, resentments, and shocks.

- Override other people's criticisms. Opinions are just that— people say what they *think*, and often they don't *know*. They do not know the full truth about you and your motivations. The parents of Bianca's ex, had not been able to accept that their son was in the wrong.
- Act on your own behalf, not for the sake of others. If you take any action, take it to help solve the problem, not to try and tell others something about yourself.

Bianca refused to let her in-laws or school friends deflect her from caring for her family. She was not making her choices in order to conform to their expectations.

WHAT WENT WELL THIS WEEK?

Going back to Galloway's two questions with which we started this chapter, Friday's atomic journey gives us an opportunity to look behind the negatives once they have been cleared out of the way. What went well? Your life is much more than painful negatives!

Positivity Values: Bear These Things in Mind

Let's look at the bedrock of positivity—our values. We continued to hold our ground and did not slip further back into negativity because we understood these truths!

- "This too shall pass," as the famous Big Book of Alcoholics Anonymous puts it (Wullie I., 2022). Everything is temporary, even these setbacks and irritations. Bianca realized that the office situation would calm down and that her son's leg would heal.
- Happiness in life depends on your attitude, not the stuff that happens to you. Bianca ended the working week with a positive outlook because she was able to greet the negatives

of the week. By externalizing negatives, we open the space for positives.

- Value the little things that are going well. Bianca loved the quietness of Friday night, being alone while listening to her favorite piano music. She loved her children. She appreciated her job. What are the little good things in your life?
- Value the people who are supporting you. Bianca needed a friend to phone, and she had one.
- Value your lifestyle choices. Bianca had good reasons to not oblige her friends, and to prioritize her children. She was aware that her role as a mother gave her meaning in life. Do you truly value your role in life?
- Negativity comes and goes. A positive mindset, on the other hand, transforms us *within* negative circumstances. It changes us in ways that can help us overcome challenges.

Positivity Patterns: Possible Atomic Steps

When you refuse to take steps in cooperation with the negative that will break you down further, you are able to enter a special relationship with the negative—a powerful friendship. Imagine yourself saying one of these things. Over many Fridays, you will have the chance to say all of them. It's a long list, but it emerges from positive responses that real people have worked out for themselves under Dr. Ralf's guidance. Scan them quickly to see what catches your eye!

- "I accept what happened, anger. But I am only going to learn how to control myself better!"
- "Hello, anger; I'm learning to control myself better. You can't trigger my fury and stop me from being rational."
- "Hello, stress, I know you're here, but you didn't hurt me. I'm still living well, and I'll become stronger."
- "What can you teach me, fear? I am not running away, and I am not hiding."

- "Hello, my enemies. I will embrace with positive vibes, like holding the shield from Captain America. I will forgive you and invite you to leave my mind. I am invulnerable."

THE STRESS OF INVOLUNTARY SEPARATION: WHEN LIFE TEARS PEOPLE APART

An area of negativity that needs special attention is when life circumstances separate people. We love these people and don't want them to think *they* are the problem. The following scenarios are all too common:

Your child got laid off from their job during Covid-19. They are forced to relocate to another city, instantly placing thousands of kilometers between you. You are deeply unhappy, but you don't want to lose your connection with your child.

So, what do you do?

Or, what about when your aging parents suddenly need more care, but you are far away? They feel sad and lonely.

What would you do?

All relationship coaches would recommend that you talk about things. Reassure your child (or your parents) of your love. Spend much time together on Skype talking through the realities and possibilities of the situation. Together, let's discover positive ways ahead.

Perhaps this book will give you the vocabulary to talk about problems, pain, and positivity. Try studying the principles, helping each other cloak themselves in invisibility from the negatives, and actively expelling negative issues.

Sometimes there are good outcomes from involuntary disconnections. For instance, disconnecting through withdrawal can help children "individuate"—find their own unique path in life. However, you can still show your mercy, empathy, and love to each other. This is all part of the process of moving from a negative mindset to a positive mindset through this simple seven-day process, which delivers lifelong benefits.

Atomic Steps in Coping With Involuntary Disconnection

- Use a cell phone to keep a connection and share your feeling openly with your distant loved one.
- Name the things that cause pain—feelings of loss, grief, or neglect.
- Meditate on those negatives from a distance in your mind. Learn how to Say "Hello, to my Negatives."
- You can greet your negative with a Meditation seating post or relax your body with a peaceful mind.
- End your "Hello" to the negative with an empowered positive statement, e.g., I am invincible!

FOOTNOTE: WHAT HAPPENED TO ME VS. WHAT HAPPENED IN ME

It is vital that we acknowledge that there are *outer causes* and *inner effects* of negativity. Both need to be addressed, but we must be careful not to *blame* ourselves for the effects on our inner selves caused by outward negatives. Bianca's mug of hot chocolate shows us that as we deal with the negative *outer causes*—arguments, conflicts, difficulties, and tragedies—we also deal with their negative *inner effects*.

Call an Inner Negative by Its Name

Sun Tzu, the military theorist and master strategist, reckons that in order to conquer an army, you must get to know (through your spies) the names of all its officers (Sun Tzu, 2013, p. 67). For example, when faced by an angry Pitbull in a park, it would be great to know its name!

This "naming" is vital because dangerous negative preoccupations get stronger the more we practice them. (Health Essentials, 2019)

We practice them when we let them crowd our headspace and mill around without any control. The good news is that we can take atomic steps to prevent giving free space in our minds to these negative elements.

Calling an Outward Negative by Name

If you keep a daily journal, however brief, it will help you see your negatives more clearly and name them accurately. Instead of ending the week with a huge, vague cloud of bad-tempered unhappiness, the specific threats to your positivity emerge with crisp definition. They immediately appear smaller. In addition, the clearer you can see the negative event or trigger, the easier it is to choose a positive step against it and away from negativity.

An unintended effect will be that the more you see the outward challenges that you faced, the less bad you will feel about yourself. "No wonder I was so angry," you will say. "That would have made anyone mad!" All of a sudden, your change in point of view will make you more positive and help you take another step on your journey

- Write down who and what has caused your negative.
- Write down how you would greet the negative in your mind, i.e., "Hello Divorce, you hurt me deeply, I cried, and I suffered a lot."
- Write down how brave your mindset is in confronting your negative, i.e., "I don't feel afraid of you. You can't hurt me. You can't beat me down."
- Write down your positive talk to the negative, i.e., "I'm stronger than you think; I am healthy and with no sickness; I lose a few pounds, but I feel lighter even of my soul."
- Write down how you will embrace your positive mindset, i.e., "I have friends and colleagues who are supporting me. They call me, come to visit me; they care about me. All the friendships embrace me. My boss loves my work, and I will continue doing my best in my career."

On Friday, we acknowledge the negative emotions, along with their causes. No blame attaches to you for feelings. The ability to visualize a looming danger is a skill that has helped humans survive from the days of caves to the days of cities. When negative emotions disrupt your life, you must be peaceful, confront them bravely, and put them in their place.

We can get rid of negative feelings (step by little step) but we usually cannot do too much about the things that triggered them. That hostile line manager will still be there on Monday. That damn horse will still bite me whenever I groom him. I cannot control when a power cut will fail to trip-start the generator, and my month's worth of experiments in the lab will be lost. You will inevitably feel *something*—and I am telling you on "Friday" that you can also be friends with that negative feeling. More than that, you can master it!

Don't try to force yourself to change how you feel immediately! Do not beat yourself up about being beaten up! Remember that even these negative elements have meaning in your life, and rather formulate the atomic steps that, after all, only you can take.

Send Those Negatives Away!

If any of these considerations shed some light in the darkness, then you can mobilize some atomic steps of gratitude. That could be your easy Friday exercise, a wry smile and a small flicker of gratitude. After all, you did survive. Be grateful for your survival, but also for so much more. Handle difficult moments with gratitude. Go back in your mind over all we have discussed from Monday till today.

Here, however, we are using a new perspective: even in a bad situation, our mindset is relaxed and brave enough to face negativity and make friends with the negativity. The powerful skill here is to confront the negativity with a smile despite the less-than-satisfactory circumstances.

Thank you for the bad situation I'm facing.

I'm watching you, bad luck!

Take an atomic step forward into a positive mindset because you need freedom of heart to enter Saturday!

Friday's atomic step is to have one small positive interaction with an element of your negative side.

Tomorrow, on "Saturday," we will take all the positive learnings of the week so far, from Monday to Friday, and synthesize them through the catalyst of celebration! We find that the more we appreciate the positive, the more positive we feel!

SUMMARY

- The first step in getting rid of negative influences and reactions is to name them by their specific names
- The five negative emotions help us to understand why we are negative and how we can become positive.
- We must understand our anger, sorrow, fear, shock, and disgust.
- Then we must send them off to a distant place in our mind to open the way for a positive weekend.
- We can consciously adopt positive values.
- We can greet all the positives from the week, and establish a contract with them to stay with you through the coming week!

SATURDAY: CELEBRATE EVERYTHING

AVA'S AWFUL SATURDAY

Ava opened her bleary eyes on Saturday morning. She wished she was still asleep as the light ricocheted around the inside of her skull. Ugh! She had drunk too much last night. "I must stop drinking," she told herself, knowing that she would never keep that resolve. She gloomily took some aspirin and drank a glass of water, while the Saturday ahead came blearily into focus. The prospect brought her no joy. She had to open her computer and do a lot of work if her team was going to meet their Monday deadline. Then she'd order pizza, watch TV, and go to bed. "Ah well," she muttered to herself as she untangled herself from the duvet and staggered to the bathroom, "let's get today over with as soon as possible."

It breaks my heart that Ava is facing two days of (relative) freedom —48 hours of creative potential—in such a bad mood. I can see that she is heading towards a negative Sunday, and an even worse Monday. I wish she could grasp the atomic principle we are going to look at on "Saturday"—celebration! Let's imagine a better weekend for her. Later.

Meanwhile, Happy Weekend! Let's celebrate!

Celebration is a potent tactic in our struggle against negativity.

Insight From "Chocolatada Navideña"

When the Peruvian government enforced a complete national shut-down for the country to stop the spread of Covid-19 in 2020, it had some disastrous consequences. It almost obliterated the small Q'ero people group, high up in the Andes, in extremely hard-to-reach villages. The supply of food-stuffs to the nearest market towns dried up, and anyway, the Q'eros were forbidden to leave their villages. They were on the brink of starvation.

Fortunately, they were quickly noticed by international aid agencies. Soon, special permission was obtained from the government, and convoys carrying staple food and clothing started creeping up over difficult roads to help out the Q'ero villages. Several NGOs carried out relief projects, but I noticed something refreshingly different about one of them, the HeartWalk Foundation.

They distributed the usual staple provisions—corn and beans, tinned protein, and warm clothing. But they also distributed every-thing the people needed to celebrate Chocolatada Navideña, an important local Christmas-time festival on 19 December. It requires a lot of "non-essential" chocolate. The sweet chocolate drink and special sweet bread would not have been on the menu that year without these expensive ingredients. The power of that celebration was astonishing in motivating the Q'ero people to keep going through hardship, and resume post-Covid life.

This NGO understood the positive power of celebration, "lighting a candle of hope in dark times" (HeartWalk Foundation, 2022).

So on "Saturday," my atomic journey focuses on the importance of celebration.

Couples celebrate "one-month anniversaries." Are they being silly? No. They are confirming to themselves and the world around them that their relationship is significant. Who said you have to do something sensational in order to celebrate? Who said it? Where is it written? One month of a loving relationship is a great thing to celebrate, and I do not begrudge them their pleasure. It cheers me up and lifts my mood, as well, so their celebration benefits me too!

Perhaps, like Ava, you are not so happy this Saturday, and you're opening up your bleary eyes upon a dreary day ahead. You are so trapped by negativity that you feel like those Peruvian villagers, starving to death and unable to do anything. Well then, perhaps all you need is a bit of chocolate. You may say that I'm crazy. Can you celebrate your unhappiness? I can't guess at the details of the unhappiness you have encountered. A Zen state of mind, however, can help you capture the paradox of suffering and joy and emerge with tranquility—and celebration. Once you can celebrate your unhappiness, you are at a level of positivity where you can see that everything has meaning in itself. You are confused at this moment. However, soon you will understand, in a week, a month, a year, or a couple of years.

Let me bump you out of bed and suggest that it's only because you haven't looked properly that you haven't seen all the things you have to celebrate! Here's a taster:

- Treat yourself to a beer at the start of the football season!
- Eat a cupcake with a knife and fork to celebrate Bastille Day.
- Buy a burger and eat it off a Versace plate, and pour coke into a champagne flute. Cheers!
- Take your kids to the park, buy them ice cream, and tell them you're celebrating Saturday!
- If you are an introvert, celebrate Saturday by having a morning in the public library or a morning with your cat!

Saturday's atomic step project is all about telling yourself that your life is significant, and our journey promises to take you to a place where you can make your life more interesting, even if you celebrate alone. You do not need a big budget. Just find some silly reason to celebrate. Make life colorful.

HOW TO CELEBRATE

The first thing to get out of the way is that you do not have to have a birthday, a graduation, or a major festival in order to celebrate. In fact, little celebrations can be a lot more fun—there are no expectations from anybody and no major logistical efforts to make. Post-Thanksgiving depression is a thing! (MacCarthy, 2021)

Nobody is going to criticize how little you spend on it. Nobody will be upset because they were not on the guest list. Saturday is the day to enter the world of everyday festivities!

Celebrate Imaginatively

A Welsh family got caught in a massive flood in Indonesia once. The parents worked for an NGO, and the children attended a local school. They were trapped in their home by the water for a week, and they and their neighbors would chat across the street, which had become a river. They rigged up a pulley system with other homes so that they could share food. When the floods went down, the sweeping out of water and silt from all the downstairs rooms began, and in the midst of all that, an elderly Chinese neighbor picked his way over the debris. The husband of the family brought out two wooden boxes and then made a pot of tea. They often drank tea together before the flood. So, there they sat, in the middle of the havoc left by the retreating water. The muddy former rugby player, and the elderly Oriental uncle were sipping lovely tea from tiny cups and chatting about this and that.

It was a celebration to be remembered!

Imagination makes celebration possible under almost any circumstances! You can celebrate the anniversary of the moon landing or Star Wars Day (May 4). My computer tells me that it's some other international day whenever I open it in the morning—celebrate

International Puppets' Day, National Comic Books Day, or International Megalodon's Day! Celebrate your contribution to the ice-cream industry (most valuable client!) or celebrate your mother tongue day.

I think you must have caught on by now.

Celebrate Lavishly

There comes a time to spend all the money you can spare on celebrating. Even at a less-than-wedding scale, sometimes it's good for your mood to splash out. Why not buy a whole salmon and cook up a *Salmon Bisque* to celebrate your student child's return from university for the holidays? Or make s'mores dipped decadently in expensive melted chocolate over a fire in the backyard (at the other end of the culinary scale!) Buy a bottle of ridiculously expensive *Cheval Blanc* and celebrate, I don't know, White Horse Saturday? Korean barbecues and Japanese sushi bars also count as lavish. Depending on your budget, a whole bucket of fried chicken might be in order.

The Germans understand the concept of spending lavishly on some ordinary event—they spend a whole month celebrating *October*!

Celebrate on a Budget

Of course, we cannot always completely empty our bank accounts —that only leads to another sort of negativity. You can, however, turn a packet of Graham crackers into a treat shared by you and your grateful dog! Ice cream is always a celebration of creamy coldness. Sometimes a walk in the fall, leaning into a fresh breeze on the way out and then letting the wind blow you back home, can be the perfect celebration of the turn of the seasons.

A friend of mine used to take his kids along to watch the piglets through the gate of a nearby farm. Any little acknowledgement of gratitude or interest can because for celebration.

Celebrate With Company or Without

Invite friends. If they don't come alone, celebrate! If you are a tennis fan and the annual tennis jamboree is taking place at Wimbledon (and you are on another continent), why not buy a small punnet of strawberries and a little tin of cream? You can eat them in front of your TV with a cup of Earl Grey tea and celebrate the "tennis-ness" of tennis.

If you are more on the sociable, extroverted side, of course, you might *need* friends and family around for celebrations. Attract them in by the craziness of your suggested celebrations—become known as somebody who finds excuses to celebrate! Perhaps your craziness will spread, and others will get caught up in Celebration Saturdays too, and then you will have spread positivity around you in a widening circle. Of course, we can bring more celebration into our lives any day of the week for positive effects, but Saturdays are my day for delving into this topic and exploring how important this expressive action is for developing a positive mindset.

CELEBRATE THE EXTRAORDINARINESS OF LIFE

I have already touched on this in the "how to" section, but it is important to stress that you will feel much more positive about life if you actively celebrate the extraordinary events of life. Do not hold back. A good celebration well celebrated will crank up your inner positivity ratings. In addition, extraordinary occasions are perhaps more common than you might think.

Celebrate Beginnings

So many people are celebrating pregnancies on social media now. Baby bumps are a thing. Some parents-to-be run nine months of reports, labeling the woman's growing belly. All I can say is that the beginning of a new life has to be worth making a fuss over. On the other hand, you may not have the privilege to be celebrating anything new in your life, and you may be feeling totally not in the mood for partying, even on the smallest scale.

You can, however, celebrate that your positive mindset has started to open—even a tiny bit. Mark the date on your book (paperback) or make a note in your journal when you start to learn from this book. You have a new beginning to celebrate.

There is an immense range of new beginnings to celebrate, and different cultures have unique celebration protocols. Weddings celebrate the beginning of new marriages. Ships get launched with champagne or fireworks. Buildings and bridges have ribbon-cutting rituals. New Years are celebrated by different cultures at a number of different points on the international calendar. All these, however, usually come with fairly rigidly inbuilt celebration expectations, even down to specifying certain foods and drinks. I certainly would encourage you not to withdraw yourself from such festivities. Often, these are times when we can relax our inhibitions a little, and by and large, they help to pull us towards the positive side of life. They celebrate gratitude for the closing season and thankfulness for the potential of the new one.

In our everyday lives, there are many personal "beginnings" to celebrate. New school years and new school terms, first days in kindergarten, primary and secondary schools are all occasions that are worth marking with an extra largesse. First days in college and first days in new jobs are also important life changes. The first drive in a new car is worth a party. But in the spirit of a grateful life, one could celebrate new shoes, a new computer, the earning of a driver's license, and many more hopeful beginnings.

A celebration imbues the new with positive expectations and curbs any anxiety that might come with novelty.

Celebrate Endings

Endings are also worth celebrating. Teachers should party hard at the end of the school year—these are people who invest their lives in others and receive relatively little reward. The teaching year leaves educationalists exhausted, and if you are a teacher who is struggling with negativity, you ought to be looking for elements in the stress to celebrate. In many cultures, there is a special celebration attached to the finishing of the roof of a new building. Sportspeople typically celebrate the end of each match they play, whether they win or lose. In the American education establishment, there is an odd double-celebration of the end of a student's studies—first the oddly named "commencement" ceremony, followed by "graduation." These are all what cultural anthropologists call "rites of passage," celebrations that mark the end of one phase in life, and the transition on to the next. Funerals are often referred to as ceremonies "celebrating the life" of the deceased. All this is designed to help us transition peacefully and positively from one stage of life to another.

On a more personal level, our private lives should have peacemaking "ending rituals." Sundowners end a day for some, and evening prayers fill the same function for others. Weekends have their own rituals of closure as people head out to the pubs and clubs or churches, mosques, and temples. If you are struggling with life, you should consider setting pleasurable little traditions in place for the end of the morning's work, the end of the day's work, and the end of the week's work—little signs that life is progressing and that you are not stuck where you are.

During weekdays, you can celebrate when you have knocked off for the day. Have a glass of beer or a margarita before heading home.

Celebrate Ongoing Projects

Often I forget the ongoing sources of peace, happiness, joy, contentment, and satisfaction in my life! Running through all the negativity that swirls around me are these cables of positivity that anchor me to a positive future! I celebrate them. Saturday, as our day of celebration, does not miss out on these elements as we move along our atomic journey.

Are you in a steady job that pays your bills and funds your lifestyle? That deserves a trip to the burger shop with your kids occasionally. "Come on everyone! Let's go to McDonald's! And do you know where the money comes from? My job!" This strengthens your positivity as well as teaching your children the value and wonder of work. On the other hand, perhaps your job is more than just a paycheck—it's your life's passion. A member of a medical research team has little things to celebrate with family, friends, or even just the dog! The promising look of the new enzymes can be celebrated. The success of contact-making at the recent conference is worth a focused treat.

Don't waste all your treats on "comfort foods" when you are feeling down—that way, you are only reinforcing negativity! Switch your snack eating habits to when you have something to celebrate! So, even if you are feeling down, find some scrap of positivity to celebrate. In that way, you are providing sensory affirmation of the positive, rather than rewarding the negative.

Another ongoing project is your life, with all its potential! That is worth the occasional festive affirmation! Your good health is another. Your five senses are great things to celebrate—you could have a "celebrate sight" day or a "celebrate hearing" day (when you go to a symphony concert or play your favorite jazz through your iPhones).

Saturday is when we take the gratitude steps from Tuesday and make a fuss of them! We not only value things for ourselves, but we draw the rest of the world in to share them with us. We spread positivity, and that spreads positivity inside us even more.

Celebrate Weird Occurrences:

A $20 note once blew up against me in the Toulouse traffic! Weird, right! Of course, I grabbed it! And then what did I do? You guessed it, the whole family went down to the ice cream shop! If anything unusual happens, celebrate it. Even if it's something terrifying like an earthquake, which is a reality in many parts of the world. Celebrate an earthquake with jelly to cheer up frightened children. The next time a tremor hits, you can say, "Oh, we're going to have some jelly again tonight!" and I guarantee that will help everyone feel less scared.

There are many other oddities that can be celebrated. If you see a red, blue and yellow car together in the traffic, that's a good reason to celebrate with Smarties (or M&Ms!) If there's an eclipse, why not come home with sunflowers? If your team ends up on a disappointing losing streak, then commiserate with donuts!

I can't list all that many weird occurrences you could celebrate, but you'll recognize them when they happen!

Celebrate Interesting Developments

We have already noted that pregnancies are a good focus for celebration. How about the new album your favorite artist has just dropped? You can celebrate by dancing to your headphones all day (or whatever seems appropriate). If you are a miner working kilometers underground and you stumble on a promising new seam of gold, that calls for pit-head celebrations. If your best show-dog has a litter of puppies, break out the festivities—the next Crufts champion might have arrived in your home! If your supervisor asks you mysterious questions about how you might fit into the organization at a higher level, celebrate the interest management is taking in you.

It is important to celebrate things *before they are complete*. Some people are afraid to "jinx" things with premature celebration. However, if we hold off our enjoyment of the process, it means we only think we deserve anything if we finish something. That is not true. It is a negative assessment of yourself to think you only deserve celebration once you have completed an achievement. It is also an achievement to be working toward a positive outcome. Let's draw down on future good vibes en route to the winning tape!

Celebrate Important Relationships

All around the world, there are formal, socially acceptable occasions for celebrating the existence of family and friends. Wedding anniversaries are formally celebrated with gifts (in some Western cultures) ranging from paper to diamonds, depending on how many years the marriage has lasted. Birthdays are usually celebrated, with an emphasis being placed on all the multiples of ten (starting with 30!) or twelve (12, 24, 36, etc.), with a particularly lavish feast on the 60th birthday. In other cultures, 15 is especially significant; in others, it is 16, 18, or 21. There are also different ways of celebrating Mother's Day, Father's Day, and Teachers' Day around the world. These should not be ignored or skimped on. A relaxed celebration featuring praise and appreciation, will go a long way towards turning negativity into positivity.

On our atomic journey, however, we need to develop our capacity. An unexpected bouquet of flowers, chocolate, a book, or some other thoughtful and useful gift on an occasion that is *not* a formal celebration day is going to turn an ordinary day into a day of celebration and appreciation. Celebrating a person not for what they have accomplished (another year of life), but for who they are, affirms an important truth—this person is not important to you because of what they *achieve*, but because of who they *are!* Random celebrations communicate unconditional love and are especially important in family relationships that have lost some of their initial positivity.

There are so many ways of celebrating the people in your life, lavishly or on a budget. Saturday's atomic step for you could be thinking of someone you want to celebrate and deciding how you can do it. Buy flowers or chocolate for someone who has helped you a lot. Dish out a cupcake to the doorman of your building, just for fun? If you are a rubbish collector, wear the fairy wings you found in someone's garbage! Treat life differently because you want to celebrate its value!

Celebrate Important Memories

It is also important to celebrate past events and people you remember. Sometimes these things are a focus for remembered grief and sadness and lower our mood. The celebration of the lives of friends and family who have died can shift our moods from one of sadness to one of gratitude. Some cultures in the East and Middle East, especially, have festival times devoted to tending graves and remembering the generations that have gone before. A Westerner might consider that morbid at first glance, but it is not so. It is acknowledging the negative in order to celebrate life.

Latin America recognizes this need as well, with their *Dia de los Muertos* carnival traditions. Candles are reverently lit for the departed, and then the party begins—the same party that you used to celebrate with those you love. Once more, these formal celebrations are wiser than we are—we who rush through life neither shedding tears nor laughing, and become locked into negativity. Positivity does not emerge from denial of grief, as we have already observed in our Friday reflections.

So, how can we benefit from little celebrations of memories? Sip a beer in memory of your father as you watch a baseball game. Read a book that your granny read and re-read. Drink the sort of tea your friend always drank, and let the subtle aroma draw out grateful memories of happy times.

We do not only celebrate those who are deceased, however. There are other important events in our past that will provide positivity through celebration. A couple can revisit the place where the marriage proposal was made and accepted—classic romantic nostalgia, and almost certainly effective in reviving memories of the euphoria of love, which are powerful positivity stimulants! Open the file on your last overseas trip and relive the sights and sounds of your holiday. Read to your grandchildren a book you read to their mother or father when they were toddlers. Play that music you raved to in your twenties.

Ava's Better Saturday

I promised that I would return to Ava's awful Saturday predicament, so here we are. What would Ava's day look like if she absorbed the concept of a Saturday celebration?

Ava opened her bleary eyes on Saturday morning. She had a bit of a headache, and the light was very bright. She smiled to herself. She had drunk too much last night, but it had been such fun to hang out with her friends! "I must stop at two drinks," she said to herself, "like I usually do." She knocked back a couple of aspirin in a tall glass of water. "Ahhh," she murmured, "it's going in pure, and it'll take all the poisons out with it." She reflected for a moment with pleasure on the healing power of water. The day lay before her, full of interest and promise. Then she remembered the work she still had to do to meet the team's deadline on Monday. "It's been so interesting," she said to herself. "I really enjoy my job! And this project will get us a big bonus!" She spent some pleasant moments imagining the new car she would be able to afford on the strength of that Saturday's work. "If I work hard, I'll be finished by six," she thought. "Then I can either order pizza and watch a movie on Netflix, invite some friends over, or go out. I won't decide yet. I'm so grateful for a whole weekend to unwind in!"

Which weekend would you like? Ava 1 or Ava 2? You can choose either!

As Oprah Winfrey has said, "The more you praise and celebrate your life, the more there is in it to celebrate" (Feeley, 2014).

Saturday's atomic step is to consciously celebrate one great thing about your life.

I am always astonished by how many good and positive things I discover in my life—when I allow myself to view them and refuse to be dominated by negative thinking. "Sunday" then sets the tone for the resolution of the negatives of the week and the establishment of a positive platform from which to launch the next week's journey.

On Sunday, we connect with our world through all our senses and emerge refreshed.

SUMMARY

- Celebration is a powerful tactic for bringing positive outcomes from negative circumstances—even if we are unhappy, there are still things to celebrate.
- Celebration matches festivity to gratitude.
- There are many ways to celebrate—imaginatively, lavishly or on a budget, and with or without others.
- There are many reasons to celebrate—beginnings, endings, ongoing projects, weird occurrences or interesting developments, important relationships, and important memories.

SUNDAY: EXPLORE THE INNATE POWER OF OUR FIVE SENSES

I s it a good morning, though? Or are you hitting the same notes as Steffy?

STEFFY'S SUNDAY

Steffy was struggling to stop working. "At least nobody can say I've got a poor work ethic," she thought to herself one Sunday. She worked from home, so she was sitting at her computer in the home office she had set up on her dining room table during Covid-19. Her boss was quite happy for her to never come back into the office once the restrictions eased. Her output was prodigious. Steffy herself was more than happy to work from home without wasting time on a daily commute, coffee breaks, or trivial interruptions by colleagues. Steffy really liked to work.

Steffy did not like much else about her life. She had not seen any of her friends for months. Her gym membership had lapsed because she had not exercised for so long. She ordered her groceries online and most of her meals, too. Her weight was going steadily up, and she seldom got out of her pajamas, except when she had to dress up for an online meeting. She didn't have enough energy to do much housework, and all the plants in her herb garden had long since died. She wrapped herself in her work, from when she woke to when she got too exhausted to stay awake at night.

When she did sleep, she did not get the refreshment she longed for as she tossed and turned, drifting in and out of shallow sleep filled with ominous dreams. She would often lie awake, longing for dawn. Sometimes she got up in the deep darkness and worked away at her current work project, her face lit by her computer screen.

Steffy could not remember when she had last put in for leave. "I don't want to go anywhere," she muttered, "and this work isn't going to do itself." Day blurred into day as she labored on. Weekends blended seamlessly into weekdays, and she worked as close to 24/7 as possible. Lately, she had been bursting into tears for no reason.

She had been filling her life with work and avoiding her friends, so she was startled that Sunday when the doorbell rang. It was her best friend, Pam. "Oh, hi," said Steffy unenthusiastically. "I'm really busy at the moment, Pam."

"On a Sunday? Nonsense!" said Pam crisply. "Open the gate and let me in!" Steffy buzzed her into the lobby of the apartment block and waited resentfully for her friend to ride the elevator up to her floor. Pam bustled in like a spring wind.

"Where have you been, Steffy? We've all been worried sick about you!"

Steffy grimaced. "I've been tremendously busy," she said. "There hasn't been any time to socialize, I'm afraid."

Pam looked around at the state of the apartment. She took note of her friend's baggy pajamas and unkempt hair. She realized that her friend was in deep depression. "Would you like to talk?" she asked gently. Steffy burst into tears.

Later that day, after a long conversation, Steffy and Pam left the apartment block arm in arm. Steffy had been crying a lot, and she was wearing her darkest sunglasses. Pam was saying, "...so you don't need to suddenly change your mood completely, Steffy. Just take a small step towards positivity, and don't judge yourself for where you are. I'm certainly not judging you."

The two friends stopped outside a small shop called "Uncommon Scents." "Let's get you a new perfume," suggested Pam. "I always find that a new perfume cheers me up."

Steffy and Pam went into the little store, and started working through the scent samples. "What's this one called?" asked Steffy eventually. "It's very fresh. I like it."

"It's called L'amour, from France," the shop assistant answered.

Pam whispered to Steffy. "This is not L'amour from now on. You can name it COURAGE! Then, whenever you wear this perfume, you will be enveloped in COURAGE. In fact, why not rename all your perfumes? You can choose any fragrance you like and name it with a positive term!

The golden afternoon sunlight engulfed the two friends as they strolled by the canal-side. Steffy felt strangely lighter. The feel of the wind stirring her hair, the sound of the starlings chattering, and the beauty of the early spring leaves made her feel better than ever before. "Let's eat at the Italian Restaurant!" she suggested.

Pam smiled.

Our atomic journey has wound its way to "Sunday," and this scenario reminds us how important it is for us to take the steps into positivity seriously. I am not asking you for dramatic changes—just little nudges and small adjustments, all in the direction of positivity. I certainly know the attraction of working straight through one week and into another, and the one beyond that too. Sometimes it is unavoidable. Our bodies, minds, and spirits, however, crave rest and recreation.

So, how can our journey of atomic steps help us to not fall into the all-too-relatable situation that Steffy faced? Sunday is a day for practicing techniques and insights that can bring us moments of refreshing rest on the busiest of weekends, and on all the other days of the week.

God created the world very actively for six days, and then he took a deep breath and rested. He probably spent the day hanging out with Adam and Eve in their yard. In the Hebraeo-Christian Insight Tradition, God made people in his creative image, and so a week of creative work is also gifted with a day of rest.

Sunday is, if at all possible, a day for relaxing. Other cultures and religions have different arrangements for ensuring breaks and holidays, but the atomic path has taken us through six days, and here we are on a day of rest—any designated day of rest. If we are not on holiday (and perhaps feeling negative about that), imagine that we are relaxing on our couch, in a garden, or on the beach. Go find a good seat at Starbucks to do some people watching or even some people-sketching. Let's use the best tools we have for positive imagination, our five trusty senses of smell, touch, taste, hearing, and sight. They will guide us into the ways of recuperative, positive thinking. Why five senses? How? Let me show you.

Have you ever heard a sound or smelled a scent that instantly and unexpectedly transported you back into a happy place in your memory? The smell of freshly cooked rice, perhaps, or roast potatoes, or that scrumptious staple of the Northern English diet, Yorkshire puddings! It doesn't have to be food—the same happens with a cardigan I haven't worn for a long time, or a blanket that has been unused for a long time and has picked up the cedar aroma of the cupboard, and the softness of the wool takes me right back to cold Christmases and warm living rooms. I found a perfume I bought years ago, on my first trip to Paris. It had lain, forgotten, at the back of a drawer. I unstopped the delicate glass stopper, and instantly all the good memories returned.

This "sensory memory" sometimes happens to me unintentionally, but I have found that positivity often floods over me when I shut down my keyboard for a moment and consciously allow my five senses to lead me.

Social anthropologists talk about our "worldview," the innermost core of our consciousness, which consists of all those things we assume are true—so obviously true that they do not need argument or explanation (El-Aswad, 2022). This is the part of us that is deeper than thought, feeling, or reflection. It is the constellation of factors *by which* we think, feel and reflect. The five senses cut through all our plans and reasoning and connect us with this deepest part of ourselves.

Five Senses and One-Second Flashes of Clarity

I want to introduce you to a way of sensory meditation for a busy person. Many of you are so stressed that you cannot imagine going through the usual steps of settling into a quiet space and so on. Life has endless noise, no private space, and random demands coming at you with relentless urgency. A surgeon experiences life like this, as do all medical personnel. First responders, as well, can rush through stressful days with no opportunity to rest. On occasion, my business demands have put me in such a situation.

Here is how I have coped. I have primed my senses to work for me to provide instants of recollection, by which I mean one-second flashes of mind-space clarity. I think of them as five triggers for positivity, and they salt my business day with the promise of tranquility beyond the stress—I "Sundayfy" my weekdays if you like. This approach works because our senses are wiser than we are and are powerfully at work to help us manage ourselves in our environments.

First Steps in Sensory Meditation

Why the five senses? Our senses are always with us, even for those of us who, sadly, have no sight or hearing. We cannot be alienated from the senses we have in daily life. On Sundays, we might focus on tapping into our senses, but all through the week, we carry their potential with us to unlock the chains of negativity. The senses remind you anytime, anywhere, that you can associate them with your daily practice!

Empowered by Sight

Begin with gratitude. If you can see, you have a great gift that can fill your inner being with knowledge, pleasure, and positivity. Beauty comes to most people first through sight. On the Sunday of our journey, we consciously recognize and use sight as a force for good.

Be open to visual cues for moments of mindfulness. *See* a weed pushing up through a crack in the sidewalk? *Notice* the sun's ray cutting across the shadowed background. *Observe* the colors on a pigeon's wing. *Note* the harmony of a beautiful building. None of these needs to occupy more than the tiniest fraction of your day. There are still 86,399 seconds left in Wednesday for you to meet your urgent deadline or get emergency surgery.

Look *into* your reflection in a mirror, not just *at* it. What you see in the mirror is more than a physical "you." You can see that you are smiling in the mirror, even if you are not smiling physically. Visualize a confident, unstressed person, and self-talk that to yourself. Stop weaponizing your reflection to reinforce your negative opinions of yourself.

Lose yourself for a moment in the deep clarity of the blue sky on a fine day. Soak your computer-reddened eyes in a cool vista of steady rain. Find a smog-free night sky and let the crowded stars speak clarity to your mind.

There are so many positive triggers in this world. Wander through a museum and ask yourself, "Which painting stirs me most deeply?" Go back and spend a little time staring at the artist's brushstrokes and enjoying the balance of colors and shapes. Thank the artist inwardly for catching this vision for you.

Your eyes can bring you a lot of pleasure—it all depends on where you let your gaze linger. That's why sometimes you should ration your viewing of TV news, which specializes in upsetting imagery because bad news sells better than good news. Psychologist Tom Stafford reckons that "journalists are drawn to reporting bad news because sudden disaster is more compelling than slow improvements" (Stafford, 2014). Sunday is a day to resist that compulsion, turn off the TV, and fill your physical vision with floods of beauty and good humor. Read a positive book. Watch a funny movie. These things will drag you out of sorrow. Let your gaze get lost in the greenery of a tree—if it's possible, lie under a tree and look up through its multi-layered complexity and count the shades of green you can see!

Watch children playing in a garden or on a beach. Children have a lot to teach us about the simplicity of play and pleasure, and they take us back to less troubled years.

Empowered by Hearing

If we have hearing, that too, is a deep source of help in our journey of small steps into positivity. As with any other sense, we approach our hearing with intentionality. Be grateful that you can hear even your heartbeat and your breathing.

Sometimes, very rarely but exquisitely timed, a moment of silence falls amongst all the random noise of a food hall or shopping center. These are cosmic anomalies. I remember some of them quite vividly. One happened at Changi Airport. The fleeting instant of silence fell, and I heard the sound of water trickling through the bamboo in one of their wonderful indoor gardens. What a gift! Then the phone rang, my business partners went onto the fifth point of our plan, and my flight appeared on the board—but my day was transformed by that golden instant, and I still carry it with me.

There are other powerful ways our hearing penetrates our negativity. A scrap of music. Raindrops on a roof. Even the sound of your own voice, measurably, soothingly self-talking, can be just the sensory gift you need. Watching and listening to the right sort of YouTube video can also bring positivity into your life, whether through a wise TED talk, an ASMR whisper, or the beauty of the music you love. Taking atomic sensory mindfulness steps on Sundays primes us to receive these little presents from the universe.

Spend some time in a park or sitting on a bench in an open playground while kids run around screaming, laughing, or crying. Meditate on these sounds. Do they know you, or can they bring you somewhere? Maybe all these innocent sounds can recall your memory of the simplicity of a child's mind.

Empowered by Smell

Our noses are incredibly powerful at opening up instants of recollection for us. Most of us (who are not wine or coffee connoisseurs) do not think about what we are smelling, even though we are smelling something all the time. That means that this astonishing sense works almost exclusively through the old instinctual hindbrain, connecting directly to our primal emotions. On Sundays, our atomic journey allows us to "stop and smell the coffee," as the popular saying goes. We usually mean that we should stop deceiving ourselves. I like that. I believe that our sense of smell does wake us up to hidden realities.

Smell can take us back to your childhood breakfast table—the smell of coffee from your father's cup, and the smell of toast or cornflakes. The freshly baked croissant in the bakery takes you back through all the croissants you ever ate, reminding you of a long history of simple pleasures.

The smell of approaching rain can sweep us briefly into a mountain plantation. I find my sense of smell is the one I least have to work on. My day is frequently richer because of some unintended mindfulness of the greater world behind and beyond me. One simple second has dropped a pin in the map of my frantic consciousness, showing me the way to find tranquil positivity.

As an exercise in taking an atomic step, you could choose a fragrance that represents confidence and strength for yourself. It could be an expensive fragrance from Tom Ford or Dior—or it could be a more economical brand that can be sprayed onto your skin (or your wallet if you're allergic). Nobody needs to be locked out of this olfactory experience, no matter how tight your budget might be. You can relabel the fragrances in your home with positive concepts like CONFIDENCE, HAPPINESS, or POSITIVE ENERGY. When spraying the perfume on you, the smell will then enfold you in your personal aura of CONFIDENCE! A shower gel that makes you feel positive and confident whenever you take a shower is just as bracing for your positivity. Call your lavender shower gel CONFIDENCE. That way, whenever you step out of the shower, you are embracing CONFIDENCE Nobody can stop you from being deeply stirred by the heady scent of roses or jasmine, either. You could take a detour to pass by a flower garden and enjoy the wild fragrance every day.

Empowered by Touch

Touch is an underrated sense for mindfulness, and yet it is as powerful as any other for enhancing our well-being and all-round positivity. Touch both reassures us of the presence of significant things, and helps us to give and receive positive connections in interpersonal relationships. The caress of a lover or the rough fist-bump from a friend are both as important in those relationships as any word we speak. On Sunday, our journey makes us mindful of this sense.

Close your eyes and lightly stroke your left palm with your right fingertips. Now. Are you feeling the stroking through your left palm or through your right fingertips? This little experiment shows how complex our sense of touch is. It is not only there to enable us to find the stapler at the back of the drawer!

The coolness of metal or fine porcelain can bring coolness to a heated mind—just a single degree centigrade, perhaps, but enough to remind you of the coolness of snow-covered ski slopes. The grittiness of sand between your toes on the beach, or the cold slap of the ocean over your feet—all these are Natures gift of positive power through touch. Take atomic steps towards these small disturbances of normality that otherwise flow around you unnoticed.

Living touch is very important to our wellbeing. Hug someone you love, stroke your pets. Your fingertips lightly touching their sleeve will bring a tiny positive charge into the difficult conversation you are having with a client. Or maybe an intimate partner places their hand on your shoulder while you are struggling with a phone call. Positivity flows in through those little instants. In these post Covid-19 days where some people are still nervous of interpersonal contact, make the most of fist-bumps for elevating your mood.

Touch a leaf or the stem of a plant. I have been mocked for touching trees in a park, but I don't care. I have to be responsible for my own positivity. Other people are free to remain locked into negative cynicism. There is something significant about close contact with the rough bark of a tree that has lived for four human generations.

I recommend that you embrace a tree (look out for ants, spiders, or sticky sap first!). Nature has put a 100-year-old being in your path. It gives scale to our human lives, and, also, there is nothing that communicates rootedness and dependence on nature like a tree. This Sunday, notice the trees in your life.

Empowered by Taste

At its evolutionary core, taste is a sense for distinguishing edible from inedible. But we have grown in complexity from our simple roots, and now taste is an open avenue for positive experiences. Our journey takes us a few steps further along the path to positivity through this sense.

The business lunch is crackling with problems, possibilities, and interpersonal conflict. Lean back in your chair and take a leisurely mouthful of the white Asparagus from Landes de Gascogne. If you give permission to your senses to help you, you will get a sudden memory of a relaxed meal in France. Somebody might say, "What are you smiling about?" irritably. You, however, have received a secret positive message about tranquility, and you are able to cut through the rising emotions with a reasonable solution that satisfies all the parties. Your taste buds did not address the problems under discussion. Your tongue, however. Did deal with your inner turmoil and negative emotion. Then your positive energy was released into the world.

Taste is also one of the senses that is more rarely explored on the path to inner tranquility. On Sunday, let us reflect on all the tastes that give us pleasure—our favorite candy or beverage, our favorite food. Be thankful for the ability of your tongue to distinguish all the different tastes, including heat and coolness. The sweetness of a peach, the sourness of a candy, the saltiness of rolled squid or beef jerky—all of these bring us positive memories and delicious expectations. The Japanese have expanded our capacity to name what we taste by explaining *umami* to us, the wholesome satisfaction in broth or sun-dried tomatoes.

If at all possible, prepare and eat food that brings you joy and satisfaction. In memory and anticipation, as well as in actual eating, this will be a week-long source of positive thinking.

Empowered by Sensory Complexity

Every time I land at Firenze Airport, no matter if it is spring, summer, autumn, or winter, the Tuscany air welcomes me back, dry or humid, sharply cold or gently warm. The sunshine gives me a shadow for company, and tells me about the grape harvest. The smell of burning weeds paints a picture in my inner being —Tuscany!

Our senses always act together to convey information from our environment. Smell and taste are intimately linked, for instance. The smell of the meal in the oven has never disappointed me, and neither has the taste of the meal on the plate! Meanwhile, although I am savoring a delicious mouthful, the smell, sight, and taste of the food are enveloping me with multisensory pleasure. It's a great shame to cram in a barely noticed sandwich half-way through a busy day. Sunday, in my scheme of atomic steps, is a day for enjoying the entire sensory palette of food and drink.

Consider the complex interplay between sight and sound. If you are down and in a negative mood, why not select a Netflix movie with a happy ending. Comedy and inspirational movies are intended to lift your spirits. If you are struggling with inner turmoil and negativity, you should not consume movies with sad or depressing themes. The world of the screen is expert at generating emotional response, and the brilliance of some directors is in their ability to leave us feeling bitter, grief-stricken, or shocked. On that point, avoid horror movies, unless you find them funny (some people do!).

Sound is the leading sense in bringing us peace and wholeness through music, although music videos add sight to the power of the musical message. This Sunday, revisit your playlist, asking the Marie Kondo question, "Will this bring me joy?" Cram your music listening for the upcoming week with music you know will help your mood stay positive. I have no particular suggestions here because music preferences are extremely personal. You are the only arbiter of what will lift your spirits! All I ask is that you consider the power of some music to lower your mood—certain genres that you love, but which you love for their melancholy sound, or certain songs that remind you of a relationship that you have lost.

Remember that silence is also an aural experience. Music cannot exist without the almost subliminal micro-silences between notes. More than that, though, a sustained, intentional silence in a quiet place might just be the Sunday activity that completely re-energizes your inner self for the week ahead. If you live in a crowded, noisy environment, consider the possibilities that a good set of noise-canceling headphones can bring into your life. The best place to find silence, for me, is in a natural environment. Out in the forest or on a mountain, the sounds of human activity are silenced and replaced with the moderate sounds of nature. Bird chatter, the rustle of the wind, the sound of streams or ocean waves—these form a constructive silence. The aural markers of human effort and anxious care are silenced by the great alternative reality of nature. The smell of autumn enfolds and releases you, just as the aroma of the maple leaves encloses the moist black soil for its winter rest and helps you release the falling leaves of negativity in your mind to make place, eventually, for spring's new growth.

Sunday is a day to immerse yourself in that in order to bring some of nature's peace with you into the next workweek.

Lastly, perhaps like me, you occasionally find yourself locked behind a computer on a Sunday, finalizing a proposal to meet Monday's deadline. Your senses can turn even this intrusion of work into your private life into an opportunity to discover sensory positivity. Visualize the keyboard as the skin of your intimate partner. Smile at your keyboard. It has become such a well-articulated extension of your capacity to express your ideas. Imagine how excited the board members are going to be at your creativity! Feel the pleasure of knowing that the work you are doing now will unlock vistas of future promotion opportunities. They love your proposal! Mobilized by gratitude, your fingers type fast without any sluggish writer's block. Enjoy the words as they materialize on your screen, almost as if they happened independently. Enjoy the melody of the chatter of your own typing, reminding you of the chirping and scurrying of little birds in a tree. Enjoy the sound you make for every letter you type.

Sunday's atomic step is to bask in the positive messages from all of your senses.

SUMMARY

- Our five senses connect us to our environment through the most primal part of our brain.
- By focusing on the different channels of sense experience, we can receive peace and harmony with our environment.
- The senses collaborate in bringing us information that can give great inner tranquility.

PART THREE
ATOMIC STEPS TO LIFELONG POSITIVITY

Part three might seem disappointingly short to you. But it must be so. We have taken a journey together for a short period of time. The rest of your life is the third part of my book, and I envision it as extending into a positive future for you as you continue to take simple atomic steps. You, the reader, get to write your own "Part 3."

CONCLUSION: LIVING THE ATOMIC PATH FOR LIFELONG BENEFITS

We started this journey in a dark dungeon of negativity. I unlocked the door for you and showed you the way out by a long spiral staircase of small steps. Can you see some light ahead? You got here by taking seven atomic steps towards freedom with a positive mindset in a world of wonderful opportunities. Well done!

Are you going to keep climbing the easy staircase? The cycle of the seven-day week is as simple as brushing your teeth.

Insight From the Nepalese Sherpas

Nepali Sherpas are famous for their capacity to carry their own weight in baggage. Westerners can typically only cope with 25% of their body weight on their backs! (Sohn, 2017)

A group of scientists recently set up a high-tech research project on the steep mountain road between Jiri and Namche to isolate the physical advantages and techniques that make Nepali Sherpas so effective. The scientists found that the Nepalis had no physical advantage over other humans. They were completely ordinary, even though they had an undeniably extraordinary capacity for shifting loads up and down mountains.

The only conclusions the scientists could come up with were, one, that they started carrying loads in their childhood. Two, they walked slowly and took small steps. They do not slow down going uphill or speed up going downhill. They walk relentlessly, tirelessly, and highly effectively (Sohn, 2017).

Positive results are achieved by ordinary people, not superhuman. Reflect on how ordinary you are and how that means that you are uniquely able to move away from negativity! Be realistic about how much weight you can actually carry, and then at least you will be able to move. Be positive about your averageness! Atomic steps are not for super-sherpas, they are for the rest of humanity like us with limited capacity!

You can achieve the positive mindset you long for, just like a Sherpa —one step at a time over a lifetime. I don't need to say more than that, really. Your potential to escape the negative and enter the positive sphere in your life is simply dependent on taking your next atomic step away from negativity. This suggests several areas in which we might consider putting in the right sort of energy (in small doses!)

Remember that nature itself intends for you to cope positively with the challenges you face. What I hope that this little one week excursion down a path of tiny steps is showing you is that you have untapped inner potential to live a happier life! There is no crushing duty for you to undertake a massive task in order to achieve positivity. Instead, there is a refreshing prohibition on effort—do "not" take difficult steps, "only" take easy ones. You were made to carry the burdens of life one small step at a time, exactly like a Nepalese Sherpa.

Insight From an Animal Wrangler

If you ever see an animal doing anything in a movie, you can be sure an expert animal handler is just there offscreen. When John Wick jumps into a taxi with his dog, the dog wrangler is lying out of sight on the floor at the back! Animal wranglers know how to get animals to do exactly what the director wants. (Geaghan-Breiner & Desiderio, 2021)

Wranglers are animal behavior experts who train spiders and cockroaches, parrots, goats, and snakes, as well as horses, cats, and dogs. They have many tricks up their sleeves, but their basic skill is an understanding of the behavior of the animal we see on the screen.

Some animals cannot be trained, but they can be manipulated by being able to predict how they will react to stimuli. Mammals and birds, on the other hand, are generally trainable, although cats are the toughest. Horses can be trained bit by bit to fall over onto a mattress (for a battle scene). Parrots can be trained to "talk" by the wrangler smearing some peanut butter into their beak—the words get dubbed in later. Wranglers train dogs by doing small step repetitions and using various treats as incentives—food, excitement, and cuddles. Apparently the hardest thing, however, is to train a dog to sit still! (Geaghan-Breiner & Desiderio, 2021)

Wrangling My Negative Inner Self

The insights for wrangling our "negative self" are invitingly close at hand. Animal wranglers employ a step-by-small-step, habit-forming training method that we must adopt. Treats are allowed! Gentle handling is essential. Understanding the nature of negativity (Friday's atomic steps) is a prerequisite. Daily, distressful repetitions are all part of it.

If you are feeling that you are "too" set in your ways to wrangle your lifetime's negative outlook, you might be thinking that "you can't teach an old dog new tricks." Scientific research has some good news for you! Contrary to the common perception that children learn faster than adults, research suggests that adults learn certain things just as quickly as kids. The only difference is in the methods they use. (Du et al., 2017)

Children go flat out learning a new skill, then nap, and then wake up knowing how to do it. Adults learn just as quickly, but they tend to analyze the skill as they go, matching it to something they can already do and catching hold of it just as quickly as a child (if you include the time the child needs to spend sleeping in the process!). Adults need to analyze. Are you exploring whether these atomic steps work for you? Are you comparing it to other books you read, or are you analyzing how this cycle works for you? It's all part of the learning process. But sometimes we literally overthink things, and our analysis leads to procrastination and paralysis. Why not take a tiny experimental step to start right now?

Do not be discouraged. You can easily learn the small skills of the atomic journey, and they can become an automatic part of your everyday life.

In the end, though, like wrangling a dog, the hardest thing to train our inner selves to do is to sit still.

ATOMIC STEPS AND LIFELONG HEALTH

Our life not only feels better when we become more positive, it actually is more healthy!

Insight From Johns Hopkins Research

Research by Lisa Yanek and her team at Johns Hopkins shows a direct correlation between having a positive outlook and having good health for life. The "pursuit of happiness" in the American Constitution can be demonstrated not to be a trivial endeavor. Yanek and her team are not certain of how the connection works yet, but people with a positive mindset are 25% less prone to heart attacks and are noticeably less inclined to "brain injury, stroke, and brain tumors" (Johns Hopkins University, 2022). She speculates that, on the one hand, having less stress means that a person will have fewer problems with inflammation. On the other hand, a positive person will be more likely to make good life decisions. Either way, positivity wins!

Yanek suggests ways of healthily increasing our positivity, which I pass on to you as potential boosters of your mood.

Vitamin Smile

Even a fake smile tricks your body into feeling better! That seems so random, but our bodies are very physical entities that do not always have to pass their reactions through the brain. Smiling relaxes us, first physically and then emotionally. Watching funny TikTok or YouTube clips is therefore *not* a waste of time—it's building up your immune system and draining stress-inflammation. When you are washing your hands in the bathroom, smile at yourself in the mirror. Smile at random strangers more often (within reason—if you are young and attractive, you don't want to send unintended signals. Specialize in smiling at very old people!) Buy tickets for a ventriloquist show or a stand-up comedy night—whatever gets you laughing and smiling. It's good for the heart.

Turn Sauerkraut Into Coleslaw

Pretend the one you don't like is the one you like. Does it sound impossible to you? Please, try! Think of all the good that cabbage must be doing for your body! Be grateful for your car instead of cursing the traffic. Yanek understands this important "atomic step" principle that we work through on Thursdays. Enjoy the extra time listening to your favorite musician without interruption. Turn "they're plotting against me" into "I wonder if they're planning a surprise party for me." "Reframe" your situation according to the most positive interpretation possible. You've got nothing to lose except your anxiety.

Positivity Protein

Practice positivity under stress and develop emotional muscle power. That is why we swing those kettlebells in the gym. The more at home we are with the dynamics of producing positivity, the better we will be when outward circumstances conspire against us. Yanek suggests three main areas to constantly work on strengthening:

- **Relationship Maintenance**. Always prioritize the precious connections you have with family and friends. When trouble comes, they'll have your back.
- **Accepting Change**. Always work at absorbing and thriving under changing conditions. In these times when it is impossible to future-proof anything, get used to riding the waves of change. You do not have to submerge your identity under the flood of novelty, but you can always salvage enough of the new technology and culture to stay afloat on a raft of new competencies!
- **Taking Action**. If you are accustomed to acting on your own behalf, you will not get caught out by not being practiced at taking action. The atomic steps I have introduced are each of them a sign to the negativity dragons that here is a hero with a sharp sword!

Atomic steps towards positivity will help you thrive in the present and press on to a better future.

The ultimate benefit of holding a positive mindset is that you have opened a new avenue into your inner being. You appreciate everything, which gives you opportunities to welcome all possibilities. You accept all the kindnesses you are offered, and you offer kindness in return. You don't suspect hostile conspiracies against you. In every way, you are now able to set yourself free from the Prison of Negativity by taking the spiral staircase of atomic steps.

ATOMIC STEPS AND FRIENDSHIP ALONG THE WAY

Insight From Marathon Running

Thousands upon thousands of marathon runners around the world run, walk, and stumble their way over the 42.195 km course. Some of them dress up as chickens. The Tokyo marathon has between 35,000 and 40,000 runners. About the same number of people run the London marathon and the New York marathon. Only a handful of elite athletes are likely to win it, with the men's race beckoning winners to finish it in about two hours and the women's winner expecting to come in at about two-and-a-quarter hours (a narrowing gap on the men's pace!) 98% of the runners know that they stand the remotest chance of winning, and are expecting to take up to six hours to complete the course. So, why do "losers" want to run so badly? The answers are an encouragement to anyone on the atomic journey!

Motivation for Getting Into Marathons (or the Atomic Journey)

Jacky Hunt-Broersma runs marathons with only one leg, using a carbon fiber blade attached to her prosthetic. She lost her leg to cancer in 2001, but now she runs marathons in around 5 hours. She recently set a new Guinness Book of World Records benchmark of 104 uninterrupted days of running the full marathon distance, over-taking the previous record of 102 consecutive-day marathons set by a woman with two legs! (Janse et al., 2022) "You're stronger than you think," says Jacky Hunt-Broersma, "and you're capable of so much more" (Lynn, 2022).

What motivates Hunt-Broersma to take one small step after another is a celebration of her recovery from cancer and an acceptance of her post-amputation body. Do you have a similar story of recovery from trauma and self esteem issues? Then the atomic journey is for you, however unfit you might feel.

Ryan Reynolds, the Hollywood "A-lister," ran the New York marathon in 2008. His father had died of Parkinson's disease, so he was raising charity sponsorships for a $100 million fund for research into curing the disease. His motivation for running was a grateful memory of his father and a visualization of a world free from a terrible disease. With regard to training, as a complete novice, his big lesson was not that he had to win the race. He had his own unique "winner's tape." "The person I have to beat is the guy I was last week," he points out (Reynolds, 2008).

What gratitude for the past or vision for the future gently motivates you to pursue the transition from negative to positive via the atomic path? If you are conscious of such elements, you will get a warm sense of approval, accomplishment, and meaning every time you take a small step on the way out of the dark.

Marathon Runners' Respect and Cooperation and the Atomic Journey

Ryan Reynolds shows us the important truth that we don't have to act as if we were being critiqued by our parents, peers, bosses, or colleagues. The atomic journey is a hidden, inner path. I am most certainly not criticizing you. You are the only spectator, and you can cheerfully cheer yourself on for what you *can* do, and not jeer yourself for what you *can't* do. Marathon runners know in advance how much they have trained, and how strong they are for uphill sections. They are very aware of their own weaknesses, but they never let that discourage them.

Respect for Others on the Journey

This leads us on to the next aspect of the inner journey that marathon running demonstrates to us—respect. Individual runners have great inner respect for their own capacities. They are also extremely respectful of their fellow runners. In sports like boxing, there is a lot of "smack talk." You never hear that on the marathon route. Runners unfailingly say a word of encouragement to others who are perhaps dropping back, or running with cramps or other pain. In the same way, it's great to be on the atomic path because that helps you feel true empathy for others who are struggling with negativity.

Cooperation with Others on the Journey

That in turn generates cooperation. In marathons, some experienced runners sacrifice their own race to run with others to finish the race in a certain time. They carry a little sign with the projected pace, and other runners can choose to run with that "bus," as they call it. A big race will have many "buses," or groups of runners who want to cooperate with others to finish in 2½ hours (fast!) all the way down in quarter-hour tranches to 5¾ hours (slow) but within the 6-hour cut-off time. Runners help each other out. If there is some crowding at a refreshment station, you will often see closer runners passing drinks to runners further away.

In the same way, when you become strong enough to help others, share what you have learned with them. Please send them this book, share your experience, and practice together—the ultimate goal, if you can, is to spread your love to others. This does not threaten you with burnout. Trying to heal others in your family or friendship circle will reinforce what you have learned and accelerate your own healing process.

Helping Others on the Journey

The cooperation in a marathon means that many of your fellow-runners are eager to help a fellow runner in distress. Ask for help! Don't feel ashamed. Every runner has known the agony of falling, grazing themselves, and then not being able to get themselves up. Runners always pick up a fallen comrade. You yourself would do this for another person in distress in a heartbeat. The micro-tears that develop in your leg muscles towards the end of a race often dictate that although you can keep your feet moving step by step, you become physically incapable of raising yourself to your feet again. Once you are down, you stay down. Watching the final stages of a marathon, when the places have been won and the stragglers are shuffling over that 42.195 km mark, you will often see runners picking other runners-up. The rules say you can't help them any further, but you can get them up on their feet again.

Since everyone understands the pain, other runners are always kind to the fallen. If you are struggling with negativity, ask a family member or friend to help you work through these atomic steps and run by your side for a while. When you are in difficult life circumstances, it's not the time to show your bravery.

On the atomic path, you might often be alone. That is no problem. Solitary life then becomes an opportunity to practice your meditative techniques that you focus on, especially on Wednesdays.

Techniques for the Journey

Runners are full of techniques they have perfected over months of training in preparation for marathon day. They consciously shorten their stride on uphill stretches, and even run gutter-to-gutter zigzags on really steep sections to lower the gradient. Runners are never deceived into racing downhill in the early stages—they know their quads and knee muscles will pay for that later. Runners stay well hydrated and know exactly what energy gels to suck in, and where to boost blood sugar levels.

By reading this book, you have achieved 50% success in changing from a negative mindset to a positive mindset—right there on the front page, I promised escape from a negative mindset to a positive mindset through a simple 7-day process, with lifelong benefits. Even though you find you couldn't absorb everything, or you disagreed with something, every small technique has become embedded in your mind. I'm sure you will practice some skills unconsciously.

You choose to read the books and find the solutions.

Now, you have almost finished your first reading.

ATOMIC STEPS CYCLE AND THE JOY OF A JUMBLED WEEK

My first hope and desire is that you walk along your own atomic path through life, and enjoy the low stress development of positivity and joy. As you gain skills and insights into your own unique inner world, I visualize you practicing the seven-day recurring approach, and that the momentum of quiet pleasure grows and flows. Eventually, I hope that you will advance so far along the path that you don't need to open the pages of this book anymore, and it gets consigned to the console table next to your bed as a memento of the beginning of your new, positive life.

I picture you finding a like-minded person who follows this path parallel to you, making their own discoveries and taking their own steps, but encouraging you to continue as you encourage them. This is not meant to be a book for solitary use. It's a textbook example of a positive community. If you spread your positive mindset, sprouts will grow! You can gift anyone you love with a copy of this method and grow together with all those who love and care for you and those you want to help. As you share your *small* successes, the process will gain power.

Lastly, there is no single formula for success. Yes, the "days" are systematically explained. But you are never going to be exactly the same as anyone else. You are unique. When you think you have grasped the essence of the seven days of practice, you can combine them into your daily practice.

You certainly don't have to apply the method by rote from Monday to Sunday. You can jump from Monday to Sunday and then reflect on Wednesday or Friday. Or, you can apply the Sunday strategy more than any other method. Any way of using this method will benefit you significantly.

Bring on the POSITIVE, and keep the ball rolling as you move from a negative mindset to a positive mindset through a simple seven-day process, with lifelong benefits.

SUMMARY

- Ordinary people gain huge benefits from taking small steps.
- Humans thrive on the habits that make life easier for them.
- As adults, we can learn just as easily as when we were children.
- Habitual positivity has lifelong positive health outcomes.
- Community solidarity provides lifelong assistance to our atomic Journey.
- It is vitally important to make the easy steps towards positivity habitual.
- Follow the steps in any order you like—strangely enough, you will still make forward progress!

IN THE TRANSIT LOUNGE

'm traveling onward. So are you. Our paths have crossed in these brief pages, and now we are choosing our unique ways forward.

As I sit in the departure lounge once more, I'm glancing over the galley proof of what I have written and making last-minute notes in the margins. It's hard to believe I have completed this labor of love. It has been a long dream, and now what I have visualized all these years is about to become reality.

My iPod is playing my usual calming and inspirational traveling songs, and I realize that I am listening to Mariah Carey and Whitney Houston singing their iconic hit, —When You Believe (Carey & Houston, 2009)

That really says it all. Frail and small though our hope might be, there are daily miracles in store for us for the rest of our lives. The song celebrates the seemingly unlikely outcome of freedom for an enslaved nation. They looked ahead, and now their faith and hope have blossomed into a new reality. The same journey is open to everyone who sets out from a negative mindset to a positive one along the path of atomic steps.

No matter how hard it is to achieve your goals or change your habits, just BELIEVE IT! Miracles will follow faith. You will be astonished one day at the atomic efforts you have made without notice. One day, at one moment, it will be in front of you! BELIEVE!

Imagine: How many people with negative mindsets refused help from friends, doctors, and family? They do not even seek help from any books for self-help. I feel sorry for them.

You choose to read the books and find the solutions. Now, you have almost finished your first reading. Congratulations!

BONUS CHAPTER

THE 8TH DAY PROCESS

DO NOTHING!

Hello, reader! I know that things have been hard for you and that you may have fallen apart or cried. By reading this book, you show that you have hope, which is good. Your bad attitude will change soon; it's just a matter of time. You've already done something good by getting this book to help improve your life. This means you are self-motivated and an entrepreneur in your inner life.

We've talked about how limited the help we can get from outside sources is. Friends, experts, and doctors only have limited options for bringing us out of negativity. I still need to lay out a list of instructions. I have confidence you can harness your situation, and I would like you to discuss my suggestions on their merits. Ultimately, your help will come from your inner resources.

So, could you hear me out one last time? It's okay not to feel okay! Suddenly, many people may have experienced downtime for no reason. Nothing can motivate them. There is no energy to practice anything they have learned, like meditation, visualization, or even going to church. You need to push yourself harder! Just relax and do nothing. Allow yourself a temporary break. Give yourself a treat— not because you have "earned" anything but because your independent thinking deserves credit. Close the book and put it next to your pillow or desk. Don't push. Whenever you're ready, please come back and open the book again.

I have no ambition to control how you think and act! You are not obliged to put these suggestions into action in any rigid order. Others may place obligations on you, but I do not. There is no guilt or performance anxiety in my journey of seven days. You could stretch out the cycle of seven days to one day per month. You could compress all seven days into a holiday weekend. You could focus on one day for a whole month, or even a year. How you use this week of atomic steps is entirely up to you, your personality, and your personal capacities. Personality-wise, I have grown into taking the small steps on the journey daily, with as little stress as deciding what I'm going to have for breakfast.

Remember, "Monday" and the other days of the "week" are just the convenient location label for the first seven atomic steps out of negativity. There is "a lot" of valuable data in each chapter, but nobody asks you to act on all of it at once! Choose one small guidance point at a time. I'm starting with Monday because the start of the working week is a natural rhythm for most of us. You can begin at any point, though.

Please remember that failure and imperfection are not only expected but also helpful. We need to change our interpretation from "I'm a failure" (you are not!) to "That didn't work," and "Let's find another way around it," or "If it doesn't work for me, let's try a different step," or even "Let's stop the week for a while and come back again later." If we treat our progress toward positivity as a scientific process, we become free to experiment and innovate. Scientists always say that a negative outcome (known as a "null result") is still a positive one because it prevents them from wasting further time down that avenue of research (Charlesworth Author Services, 2020). We need to have that same lack of ego over things that do not work out quite as we would have liked in our inner lives.

So, when you feel tired or down and don't want to take any of the seven days' solutions, relax, take a step back, and "do nothing!" No pressure here! Don't pressure yourself; refrain from negative self-talk, and do nothing if unprepared. When you *are* ready, you can come back little by little. Nobody holds a schedule in one hand and a stopwatch in the other. Nobody is writing negative comments in red ink in the margins of your life. It is "okay not to be okay!" It is a long journey, but ultimately, the atomic steps are there at your service, ready for *you* to deploy to create positive progress. We need to run only on joy, not compulsion, in any area of our life.

Another issue is the importance of being flexible and in complete control of which steps you take on and when you take them. The seven-day process is a *holistic* approach to help us change our negative mindsets *gradually*. Every part is equally valid because any situation you face might need to be addressed uniquely. Monday's practice is no "better" than Tuesday's or Sunday's, and it is not more "advanced" than Friday's. If you like Sunday more, be Ms. Sunday for a week or Mr. Wednesday for a whole week's practice. You can also mix and match the process daily. Ultimately, I hope you can unconsciously practice the process from Monday to Sunday, making it an effortless positivity skill as unnoticeable as all the traffic lights you either stop at or drive through on the way from home to work. Who remembers how many green lights and how many red lights they passed? The lights did their automatic work. You drove safely and competently, obeying the signals without stress.

With hardly noticeable repetition of the atomic steps, you will become more and more at home and adept with them. I often practice all the skills in one day. When you lie awake in bed or as you eat breakfast and commute to work, you will experience their positive influence. Your mindset will be strangely positive when you speak with your colleagues, chew your lunch, or focus at a meeting. And at the end of the day, over a drink with friends and while driving home, your positivity will radiate out, even into the traffic. At home again, in a quiet moment on your couch, playing with your kids, and in bed, visualize all the beauty of today and the following day. As the journey operates in that fashion, you will enjoy increasing positivity.

Last of all, I would like to offer you a great complimentary resource to help you get the most of the Journey of atomic steps:

"One Day of Atomic Steps - Applying the 7-Day Process to a 1-Day Practice"

You can do this by signing up for my newsletter at https://bit.ly/LConti-Newsletter

Or through my website at https://www.lawrenceconti.com/

INDEX

Insight from the Nepalese Himalayas

Insight from an Animal Wrangler

Insight from Johns Hopkins Research

Insight from Marathon Running

ABOUT THE AUTHOR

Lawrence Conti is a semi-retired businessman now working in the education sector, and the author of the Business Management series and the Self-Help series.

His work draws on his extensive experience in the business world to explore relationships and management in the corporate world, as well as the impact of mindset and how to overcome common emotional and psychological roadblocks, both in business and personal life.

Lawrence holds a degree in business management and has held managerial positions at a wide variety of companies for over 30 years. Over this time, he has made extensive business connections across Europe and Asia, broadening his understanding of many different cultures and enhancing his ability to get along with people from different backgrounds. Throughout his career, he has been required to travel extensively, allowing him to draw from business practices in other countries to shape his leadership style.

His extensive business experience has taught him a lot about handling the challenges faced by employees and managers alike, and he has worked intensively on mindset and emotional management, and how these techniques can be used to improve both business and personal matters.

Lawrence lives by the motto "La dolce vita" and has always used his business travel as an opportunity to explore and connect with other people. He loves traveling, yachting, and sampling different cuisines. He's particularly fond of Italian food and wines and enjoys cooking for his family and friends on the weekends.

GLOSSARY

APA: American Psychological Association

Atomic Steps: The one-atom high step formations on the surface of crystals.

GOAT: A popular humorous acronym for the "Greatest Of All Time," used in reference to somebody who excels in their field of expertise, often in sport.

REFERENCES

Alexander, C. F. (1848). *All Things Bright and Beautiful. Timeless Truths.* https://library.-timelesstruths.org/music/All_Things_Bright_and_Beautiful/

Al-Shawaf, L., Conroy-Beam, D., Asao, K., & Buss, D. (2015). *Human Emotions: An Evolutionary Psychological Perspective.* Emotion Review. DOI:10.1177/1754073914565518

Ames, H. (2022, June 10). *Visualization Techniques: A Guide to Unlocking Your Potential.* Dr Kiltz. https://www.doctorkiltz.com/visualization-techniques/

Anthony, A. (2019, February 16). *Sam Harris, the new atheist with a spiritual side.* The Guardian. https://www.theguardian.com/books/2019/feb/16/sam-harris-interview-new-atheism-four-horsemen-faith-science-religion-rationalism

Bareeqa, S., Samar, S., Yasin, W., Zehra, S., Monese, G., & Gouthro, R. (2021). Prevalence of depression, anxiety and stress in China during COVID-19 pandemic: A systematic review with meta-analysis. *The International Journal of Psychiatry in Medicine,* 56(4), 210–227. DOI: 10.1177/0091217420978005

Bernie Madoff: Disgraced financier dies in prison. (2021, April 14). BBC. https://www.bbc.-com/news/business-56750103

Boyes, A. (2018, August 3). *5 Tips for Coping with Regret.* Psychology Today. https://www.psychologytoday.com/za/blog/in-practice/201808/5-tips-coping-regret

Cherry, K. (2021, April 5). *The 6 Types of Basic Emotions and Their Effect on Human Behavior.* Verywell Mind. https://www.verywellmind.com/an-overview-of-the-types-of-emotions-4163976

Christensen, E. (2020, October 24). *How To Make Sourdough Bread.* The Kitchn. https://www.thekitchn.com/how-to-make-sourdough-bread-224367

Dougdale, S. (2021). *Ten tips on using the positive power of the spoken word.* Overcome fear of public speaking. https://www.write-out-loud.com/ten-tips-on-using-positive-power-of-the-spoken-word.html

Du, Y., Valentini, N., Kim, M., Whitall, J., & Clarke, J. (2017, February 7). *Children and Adults Both Learn Motor Sequences Quickly, But Do So Differently.* NCBI. https://www.ncbi.nlm.nih.gov/pmc/articles/PMC5293788/

Ekman, P. (2022). *What is Disgust? | Feeling Disgust.* Paul Ekman Group. https://www.-paulekman.com/universal-emotions/what-is-disgust/

El-Aswad, E.-S. (2022). *WORLDVIEWS: AN ANTHROPOLOGICAL PERSPECTIVE | El-Sayed El-Aswad | 6 updates | 2 publications | Research Project.* ResearchGate. Retrieved September 16, 2022, from https://www.researchgate.net/project/Worldviews-An-Anthropological-Perspective

Emotional and Psychological Trauma. (2022). Help Guide. https://www.helpguide.org/articles/ptsd-trauma/coping-with-emotional-and-psychological-trauma.htm

Fedina, L., & Latyshev, A. (2015, April 14). *Up and Down Atomic Steps # or how to pass from surface science to nanoscale measurements.* Science First Hand. https://scfh.ru/en/papers/up-and-down-atomic-steps-/

Feeley, M. (2014, June 2). *What Is the Power of Celebration?* HuffPost. https://www.huffpost.com/entry/what-is-the-power-of-celebration_b_5371668

Galloway, M. (2020, April 11). *How-to: Evaluate your week.* — LifeLeap Coaching. https://www.lifeleapcoaching.com/my-weekly-blog/how-to-evaluate-your-week

Geaghan-Breiner, M., & Desiderio, K. (2021, April 19). *How 10 Different Types of Animals Train for Film and TV Roles.* Insider. https://www.insider.com/how-animal-trainers-wranglers-train-bugs-animals-for-movies-tv-2021-3

Geggel, L. (2017, April 14). *Bushmen Painted Earliest Rock Art in Southern Africa 5000 Years Ago.* Live Science. https://www.livescience.com/58684-bushmen-painted-earliest-rock-art-southern-africa.html

Gibbens, S. (2017, February 16). *Why 'Fainting Goats' Really Collapse in Fear.* National Geographic. https://www.nationalgeographic.com/animals/article/fainting-goat-fear-response-video

Giving thanks can make you happier. (2021). Harvard Health. https://www.health.harvard.edu/healthbeat/giving-thanks-can-make-you-happier

How To Survive Quicksand. (2017, April 22). National Geographic [Video]. YouTube. https://www.youtube.com/watch?v=7CIOWh1JNTs

How to respond to negative, unexpected data and results? (2020). Charlesworth Author Services. https://www.cwauthors.com/article/How-to-respond-to-negative-unexpected-data-and-results

Health Essentials. (2019, October 3). How to Turn Around Your Negative Thinking. Cleveland Clinic Health Essentials. https://health.clevelandclinic.org/turn-around-negative-thinking/

Henzler, M. (1976). *Atomic steps on single crystals: Experimental methods and properties.* Springer Link. https://doi.org/10.1007/BF00901904

Himmelman, P. (2018). *The Power Of Positive Speech: How Choosing The Right Words Defines Your Reality.* Forbes. https://www.forbes.com/sites/peterhimmelman/2018/10/21/the-power-of-positive-speech-how-choosing-the-right-words-defines-your-reality/?sh=4caf9f6e6ea5

Humanity Unlimited Global. (2022). *Dealing with Anger: Types of Anger - Aggression.* Your Life Counts. https://yourlifecounts.org/learning-center/aggression/dealing-with-anger-types-of-anger/#

Janse, A. M., Jarenwattananon, P., & Florido, A. (2022, May 3). *Looking to set a Guinness World Record, woman runs 104 marathons in 104 days.* NPR. https://www.npr.org/2022/05/03/1095995698/guinness-world-record-104-marathons-amputee

Johns Hopkins University. (2022). *The Power of Positive Thinking.* Johns Hopkins Medicine. https://www.hopkinsmedicine.org/health/wellness-and-prevention/the-power-of-positive-thinking

Jagdish, K., Sushil, S., Fern J., Wiblishauser, M.J., & Bowman, S.L. (2021, June). Post-lockdown depression and anxiety in the USA during the COVID-19 pandemic. Journal of Public Health, 43(2), June 2021, 246–253. https://academic.oup.com/jpubhealth/article/43/2/246/6078709

Kelly, L. (2021, February 5). *The science of swearing.* Readable. https://readable.com/blog/the-science-of-swearing/

Kogan, N. (2022). *What if you do something you regret and you can't go back to change it?* Happier. https://www.happier.com/blog/what-if-you-do-something-you-regret-and-you-cant-go-back-to-change-it/

Kondo, M. (2022). *About the KonMari Method.* KonMari. https://konmari.com/about-the-konmari-method/

Lighting a Candle of Hope in Dark Times. (2022, February 6). Heart Walk Foundation. https://www.heartwalkfoundation.org/lighting-a-candle-of-hope-in-dark-times/

Lawrenz, L., & Cassata, C. (2022, April 12). *Types of Grief: Signs, Impact, Tips to Cope.* Healthline. https://www.healthline.com/health/mental-health/types-of-grief#prolonged-grief

Legg, T. J., & Gepp, K. (2020, February 21). *Fight, Flight, or Freeze: How We Respond to Threats.* Healthline. https://www.healthline.com/health/mental-health/fight-flight-freeze

Lynn, B. (2022, April 23). *Woman with One Leg Seeks to Run 102 Marathons in 102 Days.* VOA Learning English. https://learningenglish.voanews.com/a/woman-with-one-leg-seeks-to-run-102-marathons-in-102-days/6535883.html

MacCarthy, L. (2021, November 8). *Understanding Post-Holiday Depression and Blues.* Psycom.net. https://www.psycom.net/depression/post-holiday-depression

McCoy, M. (2020, December 21). *Compassion Prison Project: Transforming Prisons and Communities.* PACEs Connection. https://www.pacesconnection.com/blog/compassion-prison-project-transforming-prisons-and-communities

McCrum, K. (2016, January 8). *See the remarkable items pulled from a 200-year-old canal in Paris when it was drained for cleaning.* The Mirror. https://www.mirror.co.uk/news/world-news/see-remarkable-items-pulled-200-7138760

Mohiyeddini, C., & Beaumont, W. (2020, April 30). Swearing as a Response to Pain: Assessing Hypoalgesic Effects of Novel "Swear" Words. NCBI. https://www.ncbi.nlm.nih.gov/pmc/articles/PMC7204505/

Mubarik, A., Nartey, S., Kwarteng, E., Calys, V., Makafui, D. D., & Gantt, D. (2019, July 25). *The little-known story of how Haile Selassie became the symbol of the Rastafarian movement.* Face2Face Africa. https://face2faceafrica.com/article/the-little-known-story-of-how-haile-selassie-became-the-symbol-of-the-rastafarian-movement

McFerrin, B. (1988). Don't Worry, Be Happy. On Simple Pleasures. [Audio File]. Received from https://open.spotify.com/album/4zhRkgoZKC2xCPPys1gK4b

Outline of the Spiritual Exercises. (2022). Ignatian Spirituality. https://www.ignatianspirituality.com/ignatian-prayer/the-spiritual-exercises/an-outline-of-the-spiritual-exercises/

Point of View Shot: Creative Camera Movements & Angles. (2021, March 14). StudioBinder. https://www.studiobinder.com/blog/point-of-view-shot-camera-movement-angles/

Ralph, L. (2022). *28 Ways To Rebound When Everything Goes Wrong, From A Psychologist.* MindBodyGreen. https://www.mindbodygreen.com/articles/ways-to-rebound-when-things-go-wrong

Regan, S. (2021, May 20). *The Law Of Attraction, Simplified: What It Is & How To Use It.* MindBodyGreen. https://www.mindbodygreen.com/articles/the-law-of-attraction-simplified-what-it-is-and-how-to-use-it

Reynolds, R. (2008, November 9). *Why I'm Running the New York City Marathon.* HuffPost.

https://www.huffpost.com/entry/why-im-running-the-new-yo_b_133157

Ruth, A. (2022, January 16). *8 Ways To Train Your Brain To Become More Positive*. Due. https://due.com/blog/train-your-brain-to-become-more-positive/

Studies show normal children today report more anxiety than child psychiatric patients in the 1950's. (2000). American Psychological Association. https://www.apa.org/news/press/releases/2000/12/anxiety

Safety Tips For a Roadside Breakdown. (2014, September 15). Hastings & Hastings. https://www.hastingsandhastings.com/safety-tips-for-a-roadside-breakdown/

Satie, E. (2019, February 19). *GYMNOPEDIE Erik Satie Lyrics Words No. 1 best top popular favorite trending Wedding Love Songs Eric* [Video]. YouTube. Retrieved October 25, 2022, from https://www.youtube.com/watch?v=ltI_TB85njA

Scharper, J. (2020). *In the Heart of Darkness*. National Parks Conservation Association. https://www.npca.org/articles/2477-in-the-heart-of-darkness

Sheth, S. (2021, July 15). *Engineer designed and built his own functioning mechanical prosthetic hand and it looks like a steampunk beauty!* Yanko Design. https://www.yankodesign.com/2021/07/15/engineer-designed-and-built-his-own-functioning-mechanical-prosthetic-hand-and-it-looks-like-a-steampunk-beauty/

Sohn, E. (2017, March 12). *Study: How Do Nepalese Porters Carry So Much Weight? : Goats and Soda.* NPR. https://www.npr.org/sections/goatsandsoda/2017/03/12/517923490/how-does-a-nepalese-sherpa-carry-so-much-weight

Stafford, T. (2014, July 29). *Psychology: Why bad news dominates the headlines*. BBC. https://www.bbc.com/future/article/20140728-why-is-all-the-news-bad

Steinbuch, Y. (2021, December 30). *Retired nurse trapped in car for 5 days uses medical skills to survive*. New York Post. https://nypost.com/2021/12/30/ex-nurse-trapped-in-car-for-5-days-uses-medical-skills-to-survive/

Schwartz, S. (1988). When You Believe [Recorded by M, Carey & W, Houston]. On From the Prince of Egypt. [Audio File]. Received from https://open.spotify.com/album/0XGnvXuHiWdgB83sNrLEzX

The Damaging Effects of Negativity by Bree Maloney. (2022, January 18). Marque Medical. https://marquemedical.com/damaging-effects-of-negativity/

Tkaczyk, F. (2022). *Survival Gear List: The Survival Essentials*. Alderleaf Wilderness College. https://www.wildernesscollege.com/survival-gear-list.html

Tucker, J. (2021, August 4). *How a Sex Trafficking Survivor Escaped Her Prison*. ELLE. https://www.elle.com/culture/a36898189/0086-0088-megan-s-account-august-2021/

Velez, J. (2019). *Lady Gaga's 2019 Oscars Acceptance Speech: "If You Have A Dream, Fight For It."* GRAMMY. https://www.grammy.com/news/lady-gagas-2019-oscars-acceptance-speech-if-you-have-dream-fight-it

Verny, T. R. (2022, January 4). *Laughing Your Way to Health and Joy*. Psychology Today. https://www.psychologytoday.com/za/blog/explorations-the-mind/202201/laughing-your-way-health-and-joy

What is dissociation? (2019). Mind. https://www.mind.org.uk/information-support/types-of-mental-health-problems/dissociation-and-dissociative-disorders/about-dissociation/

Wang, R. (2022). *Yinyang (Yin-yang)*. Internet Encyclopedia of Philosophy. https://iep.utm.edu/yinyang/

Weir, K. (2013). *Feel like a fraud?* American Psychological Association. https://www.a-pa.org/gradpsych/2013/11/fraud

Wullie I. (2022). *This Too Shall Pass.* Anonymous. https://alcoholics-anonymous.eu/this-too-shall-pass/

Made in the USA
Monee, IL
23 May 2023

34439663R00116